EACH NEW DAY

WITH THE PSALMS

REBECCA RIVIERE

REBECCA RIVIERE

Each New Day With the Psalms

Copyright © 2014 by Rebecca Riviere

All rights reserved.

No part of this book may be reproduced in any form or by any electronic or mechanical means, including information storage and retrieval systems, without written permission from the author, except for the use of brief quotations in a book review.

Scripture taken from the Holy Bible, King James Version. Public Domain

Scripture taken from the JPS Tanakh 1917. The Jewish Bible (Old Testament) in English, published by the Jewish Publication Society in 1917. Public Domain

Scripture taken from the New King James Version®. Copyright © 1982 by Thomas Nelson. Used by permission. All rights reserved.

Scriptures taken from the Holy Bible, New International Version®, NIV®. Copyright © 1973, 1978, 1984, 2011 by Biblica, Inc.™ Used by permission of Zondervan. All rights reserved worldwide. www.zondervan.com The "NIV" and "New International Version" are trademarks registered in the United States Patent and Trademark Office by Biblica, Inc.®

Scripture quotations are taken from the *Holy Bible*, New Living Translation, copyright © 1996, 2004, 2015 by Tyndale House Foundation. Used by permission of Tyndale House Publishers, Inc., Carol Stream, Illinois 60188. All rights reserved.

Scripture taken from the Complete Jewish Bible copyright © 1998 by David H. Stern. Published by Jewish New Testament Publications, Inc. All rights reserved. Used by permission

Scripture taken from the Holy Bible, Berean Study Bible, BSB Copyright ©2016, 2018 by Bible Hub Used by Permission. All Rights Reserved Worldwide.

I have made every effort to contact all copyright holders

ISBN: 978-1-7358424-0-0

CONTENTS

Introduction	xi
Psalm 1:1-3	1
Psalm 2:1, 2, 7-9	5
Psalm 3:1-3,8	7
Psalm 4:2, 3; 6-8	9
Psalm 5:11, 12	11
Psalm 6:8-10	13
Psalm 7: 9, 10, 14-17	15
Psalm 8:1, 2	17
Psalm 9:1-4	19
Psalm 10:16-18	21
Psalm 11:4, 5	23
Psalm 12:5-8	27
Psalm 13:5, 6	29
Psalm 14:2	31
Psalm 15:1	35
Psalm 16:7-9	37
Psalm 16:11	39
Psalm 17:8, 9	41
Psalm 18:1-3	43
Psalm 19:14	45
Psalm 20	47
Your Thoughts:	49
Psalm 21:1-4	51
Psalm 22:1, 2; 22-25	53
Psalm 23:4	57
Psalm 24:6-10	59
Psalm 25:1, 2	61
Psalm 26:2,3,8,12	63
Psalm 27:1; 13, 14	65
Psalm 27:8	67
Psalm 28:6-9	69

Psalm 29:10, 11	73
Psalm 30:2-5	75
Psalm 31:5, 23, 24	77
Psalm 32:6-8, 11	79
Psalm 33:1-4, 6	81
Psalm 33:12, 13; 18	83
Psalm 34:8, 9; 11; 19, 20	85
Psalm 35:27, 28	87
Psalm 36:8-10	89
Psalm 37:10, 11	91
Psalm 38:21, 22	93
Psalm 39:1	95
Psalm 40:1-4	97
Your Thoughts:	100
Psalm 41:1-3	101
Psalm 42:1, 2	103
Psalm 42:7, 8	105
Psalm 43:3, 4	107
Psalm 44:23-26	109
Psalm 45:6, 7	113
Psalm 46:4, 5	117
Psalm 46:10, 11	121
Psalm 47:5, 7-9	123
Psalm 48:14	125
Psalm 49:6, 7	127
Psalm 50:10-15	129
Psalm 51:10, 15-17	133
Psalm 52:8, 9	137
Psalm 53:1-4	139
Psalm 54	141
Psalm 55:22	145
Psalm 56:3, 4	149
Psalm 57:7-11	151
Psalm 58:1, 2	153
Psalm 59:16, 17	155
Psalm 60:4	157
Your Thoughts:	159
Psalm 61:2-4	161
Psalm 62:6-9	163

Psalm 63:1-8	165
Psalm 64:1	169
Psalm 65:1, 2	173
Psalm 66:1-4	177
Psalm 67	179
Psalm 68:1	181
Psalm 69:35, 36	185
Psalm 70:4	189
Psalm 71:16-19	193
Psalm 72:17-19	195
Psalm 73:1-3; 26-28	197
Psalm 74:16	201
Psalm 75:3	203
Psalm 76:1	207
Psalm 76:7, 10, 11	209
Psalm 77:11-15	211
Psalm 78:1-4	213
Psalm 79: 8, 9	217
Psalm 80:1, 3, 4, 7, 14, & 19	219
Your Thoughts:	223
Psalm 81:1-4	225
Psalm 82:8, 3, 4	229
Psalm 83:1-6	231
Psalm 84:10 - 12	235
Psalm 85:10, 11	237
Psalm 86:1, 2, 11-13	239
Psalm 87:6, 7	241
Psalm 88:1, 2	243
Psalm 89:1-43 35-37	247
Psalm 90:1, 2:17	249
Psalm 91:1	251
Psalm 92:1-4	253
Psalm 93	255
Psalm 94:14, 15	257
Psalm 95:1-8	259
Psalm 96:11-13	261
Psalm 97:1, 2	263
Psalm 98:1	267
Psalm 99:5	269

Psalm 100	271
Your Thoughts:	273
Psalm 101:1	275
Psalm 102:16-18	277
Psalm 103:1-5	281
Psalm 104	283
Psalm 105:14, 15	285
Psalm 106:7, 8	287
Psalm 107:8	289
Psalm 108:1-6	291
Psalm 109:1-4	293
Psalm 110:1-4	295
Psalm 111:1, 2, 8-10	299
Psalm 112	303
Psalm 113:1-3	305
Psalm 114:7,8	307
Psalm 115:1, 16-18	309
Psalm 116:12-14	311
Psalm 117:1,2	313
Psalm 118:6-9	315
Psalm 119:105	317
Psalm 119:155,156,160,163, 164,169,175,176	321
Psalm 119:164,165	323
Psalm 120:6, 7	325
Your Thoughts:	327
Psalm 121:3, 4	329
Psalm 122:1, 6-9	331
Psalm 123:1-4	335
Psalm 124:6-8	337
Psalm 125:1, 2	339
Psalm 126	341
Psalm 127	343
Psalm 128:1, 2	345
Psalm 129:4	347
Psalm 130	349
Psalm 131	353
Psalm 132:13-18	357
Psalm 133	359
Psalm 134	361

Psalm 135:1, 2	363
Psalm 136:1, 2	365
Psalm 137:4	367
Psalm 138:2, 8	369
Psalm 139:17, 18	371
Psalm 140:1-3, 12-13	373
Your Thoughts:	375
Psalm 141:1-3	377
Psalm 142:1, 2	379
Psalm 143:9-12	381
Psalm 144:1,-4	383
Psalm 145:3,4	385
Psalm 146: 1-4, 9,10	387
Psalm 147:1; 11; 5	389
Psalm 148:11-14	393
Psalm 149:1 & 150:1,2; 6	395
Your Thoughts:	397
About the Author	399

This devotional could not have been begun or finished unless the Lord had granted the wisdom and the way to accomplish it. Therefore, to Him be all the praise and honor for His gift.

INTRODUCTION

With the guidance of the Holy Spirit, I have been able to fulfill a dream to bring the word of God to individual hearts. He showed me, that if I would stand on His word and give my thoughts concerning it's meaning, that I could open the door for every reader to grow in their unique understanding of His word.

This book is written as a vehicle for growth in the Lord, as the Holy Spirit gives personal revelation to the reader. A revelation that is given by the love of God, meeting the heart cry of the beloved child.

I am thankful for the support that I have received as I pondered each Psalm. I am thankful for the understanding of others as I struggled with being personally transformed by the word of God.

I am thankful for my spiritual brothers and sisters who gave me hope as I reached the end of this book. That drink of the water of hope, gave me the encouragement to finish the course.

It is with great gratitude that this book is written. It is with great hope that every reader will see Jesus Christ high and lifted up in their own heart.

Welcome to a high road of light, as the Lord gives light to a dark world.

To the Father, Son and Holy Spirit be glory, now and forever.

PSALM 1:1-3

Blessed is the man who does not walk in the counsel of the wicked or stand in the way of sinners or sit in the seat of mockers. But his delight is in the law of the LORD, and on His law he meditates day and night. He is like a tree planted by streams of water, which yields its fruit in season and whose leaf does not wither. Whatever he does prospers...

NIV

A WORD FROM ME: We are beginning a new journey through the Psalms. A new beginning is an opportunity to lay a foundation upon which we can build a strong Spiritual House. The foundation must be firmly set in the Rock or else it will be blown down by every wind and storm. Therefore, we will build these commentaries on the Rock, who is JESUS Christ and to Him belongs all the glory. JESUS is the manifestation of GOD and is the Word made flesh. In Him is all truth and from Him comes the Truth because He is the Truth.

As we begin to build on this foundation, we will look for the truth in the Word of GOD. Having found the thread of GOD-truth, we will follow that thread with references from other places in the Scripture. I will also look into the meaning of words from the Hebrew to see if there is a deeper meaning than what appears on the surface. Remember, the Holy Spirit is our teacher.

This first Psalm lays a firm foundation for all the other Psalms. It is set in the way of the LORD. The person who delights in the way and word of the LORD and meditates on his way/word has the promise of prosperity and a fruitful life. Does this mean that we are to be bound by the Law? What about Grace, which is above the Law? Are we under Law or under Grace? First, GOD does not bind us. He sets us free. Free to fly like the eagle "run and not be weary, walk and not faint." (Isaiah 40:31) if we "wait upon the LORD." Grace is the outpouring of GOD'S love, ALL of Holy Scripture is part of that outpouring (II Timothy 3:16,17) In it GOD gives doctrine, reproof, correction and instruction, everything necessary for the building of a righteous life.

JESUS showed us the understanding of righteousness, and righteous living in His Sermon in Matthew 5,6,7. When we meditate on this, we will know what is pleasing to GOD and how to live a life that is whole and wholesome. It is JESUS who sits and tells us how to be His blessed children. When we believe in Him and His Words, we will have the abundance of Grace poured out upon us. Remember: Believe in the LORD JESUS Christ and you shall be saved, you and your household. (Acts 16:31)

My prayer for you is that you will believe in JESUS, meditate on the Word of the LORD day and night, so that you will greatly pros per and bear an abundance of good fruit in your life and the life of all whom you touch.

Your Thoughts

PSALM 2:1, 2, 7-9

*Why do the nations conspire and the peoples plot in
vain? The kings of the earth rise up
and the rulers band together against the Lord and
against his anointed...
I will proclaim the Lord's decree: He said to me, "You
are my son; today I have become your father. Ask
me, and I will make the nations your inheritance,
the ends of the earth your possession. You will break
them with a rod of iron; you will dash them to
pieces like pottery."*

NIV

A WORD FROM ME: WHY? This is that universal word when we lack understanding of issues or conditions. My daughter, when she was very young, would ask, "WHY? WHY? WHY?". It would never end until she was satisfied with whatever answer I gave. Usually, in my frustration, I would say: "Because I said so, that's why!!!" This psalm shows me the patience and clarity of GOD, who is called by the Name HASHEM (Holy ONE), in Hebrew Scripture.

Our world is crying out, WHY? And the peoples are gathering together to talk in vain. The leaders of the Nations take their stand and conspire secretly, against the Holy ONE and all of His anointed. The Midrash Shocher Tov translates the first words as: Why are the masses in turbulence? "To what may the wicked be likened? To grasshoppers caged in a box who madly scramble to jump *out*."

It is to this question, that GOD answers: "You are My son, I have begotten you this day." Ponder these words from GOD to you. Son/daughter, you are the child of the Living GOD, ABBA FATHER, Almighty GO D. You are part of the family of GOD, because of the faithfulness of the Only Begotten Son, JESUS. How awesome is that!!!!

Now, GOD says: "ask of Me and I will make the peoples your inheritance and the ends of the earth your possession. You will smash them like an earthen vessel." There is no enemy that can stand in the presence of GOD, and the anointed of GOD, because GOD is our Father, and there is none greater than He. The masses will be in turbulence, and the wicked are like grasshoppers in a box, but the children of GOD will dwell in peace. JESUS IS OUR PEACE.

PSALM 3:1-3,8

O Lord, how many are my foes!
How many rise up against me!
Many are saying of me,
"God will not deliver him"
But you are a shield around me, O Lord;
You bestow glory on me, and lift up my head...
From the Lord comes deliverance.
May your blessing be on your people.

NIV

A WORD FROM ME: The world is still crying out for help. Sickness is all around and we tremble at the thought of sickness and death.

The world is crying, "How many are my foes!" "How many rise up against me!" There is fear, anxiety, grief, and torment in the hearts of the people of this world.

Many will scoff at the children of GOD, saying: "GOD will

not deliver him!" But they will be ashamed when they see the Hand of the LORD move to deliver and to save His people.

The LORD is our shield and deliverer. He is the only ONE whom we can totally trust. He knows the beginning from the end and all that happens in between. He is all knowing and Almighty.

We know that He is Almighty; we know that He is our Savior; we know that His love is from everlasting to everlasting. We know this through the evidence of His mighty work throughout all the ages. Creation is the act of GOD's Love; life and breath are His gift. He gives us new blessings every day.

We proclaim with a loud voice: THANKS BE TO GOD WHO GIVES US THE VICTORY THROUGH OUR LORD JESUS CHRIST.

PSALM 4:2, 3; 6-8

How long, O men, will you turn my glory into shame?
How long will you love delusions and seek false gods?
Know that the LORD has set apart the godly for Himself, the LORD will hear when I call to Him.
Many are asking, "Who can show us any good?"
Let the light of your face shine upon us, O LORD. You have filled my heart with greater joy than when their grain and new wine abound. I will lie down and sleep in peace, for You alone, O LORD, make me dwell in safety.

NIV

A WORD FROM ME: Look at the questions, do you hear these questions today? I know that I do. The phrases may be different, but people are asking "How long...? How long...? and Who can show us good?" We find that our trust level is slowly getting eroded by people who cannot be trusted, and we say, "How long will this go on? Who will stop them? Who can we trust to be good?"

I have had a revelation about this many years ago, and I will share it with you. When we put our whole trust in the LORD, who is the only GOOD ONE, then we can be "trusting" of others. The LORD will show who are trustworthy and who are not, this is called discernment. I sought Scriptural verification of this word and found what JESUS said in Luke 18:19 "And Jesus said unto him, 'Why callest thou me good? None is good, except one, that is GOD?'"

Notice verse 3 of Psalm 4; "Know that the LORD has set apart the godly for Himself…" Godly, in Hebrew is *hasid*, and it means the people of GOD. These are the people whom the LORD has set apart for Himself - which means, "Sanctified." Therefore, we can more readily trust the sanctified people of GOD, than those who do not acknowledge the LORD. This tells me that the bottom line must be the presence of the LORD in the heart and mind of the people with whom we associate. We cannot have an agreement, which is trustworthy, unless the LORD is acknowledged as the initiator and mediator.

When we have an agreement based on the LORD, we can rejoice and be at peace, knowing that the LORD is the only one in whom we put our trust.

PSALM 5:11, 12

Let all who take refuge in You be glad; let them ever sing for joy. Spread Your protection over them, that those who love Your Name may rejoice in You. For surely, O LORD, You bless the righteous; You surround them with your favor as with a shield.

NIV

A WORD FROM ME: I pray these verses for you and for your family. Again, we see the image of the shield, as we saw in Psalm 3:3. The NIV uses the image of the encircling shield that is "around me" and "surround me". The shield of favor, the shield of GOD around and surrounding us. This is an image which does not come from our understanding of a shield. In our experience, shields are for defense; they are round, square, or oblong; made of leather, metal or woven material. The Shield of GOD is something very different, it is the Holy Spirit overshadowing and covering the whole person.

What is this Shield that comes from GOD? It is the Shield of Faith with which the fiery darts of the wicked are quenched. (Ephesians 6:16) The NIV says: "extinguish all the flaming arrows of the evil ." What part of "all" do we not understand? Faith stands strong against the weapons of the evil one. GOD takes care of His own. Faith comes from the Holy Spirit and when we take hold of the faith, that is given to us, we are surrounded by a shield; a sleeve of protection, front, back, under, around and through.

When a person says to me that they are "under attack by the enemy," I want to say to them and to myself, "Where is your shield? Why is your shield down? Where is the hole in your shield?" The Word of the LORD is both a shield and buckler. When we stand on and in the Word of GOD, we are embracing that shield of faith. The only place where the enemy can "attack us" is in our doubt; when we pray the Word of the LORD and believe that He is faithful to His Word, we are on solid ground with an impenetrable shield around us.

I close with this word: SEEK HIS (JESUS) FACE BEFORE YOU SEEK HIS HAND then ask what you will and it will be done unto you.

Your Thoughts:

PSALM 6:8-10

*Away from me, all you who do evil, for the LORD has
  heard my weeping.
The LORD has heard my cry for mercy; the LORD
  accepts my prayer.
All my enemies will be ashamed and dismayed; they
  will turn back in sudden disgrace.*

NIV

A WORD FROM ME: Oh, it is so easy to look at these words and begin to count the enemies in our life, like they were little soldiers on a battlefield. It is easy for us to stand over them and say: "Away with you, you evil beings!!!" It is also very easy to say that these enemies are demons, lurking around trying to stab us with their swords. We are the victims of nasty, evil beings. In one case we stand over and knock away the people who do us wrong. In the other case, we feel like a victim, constantly bothered by ugly, nasty evil.

What if both of these are only a fragment of what the Psalmist is telling us? What if there is another way to look at this picture of good versus evil? Have you thought about your "thought-life"? Do you know that you are in control of that "thought-life"? You are already victorious in the battle of good versus evil without having to fire a shot. Do you know that?

The LORD has heard the cry of humankind for mercy. JESUS came to set the captives free and to break every yoke and chain of evil. With His Blood, He reconciled us; by His wounds we are healed. By the Holy Spirit, whom JESUS sent, we have access to the Throne of GOD through the torn veil. All power of GOD is ours by the Holy Spirit and we are victorious over evil, by the blood of JESUS. When we are found in Him, we are hidden from the evil one. Evil can search for us and we are hidden in the shelter of the Almighty.

I thought of this today: All good is of GOD; all evil is not of GOD; GOD is all good. It is our choice, do we entertain that which is good and live by the things which are good, thinking the thoughts that are good and dreaming the dreams that are good; or do we entertain that which is not good, and live by the things which are not good, thinking the thoughts and dreaming the dreams which are not good. That which is "not good" is not of GOD, because GOD is all good.

JESUS said: "why do you call me good, there is only one who is good, the Father who is in heaven." That Father is our Father, the Father who is all good, and Holy is His Name.

We can say in our heart what the Psalmist says: Away from me, all you who do evil, for the LORD has heard my weeping. The LORD has heard my cry for mercy; the LORD accepts my prayer.

PSALM 7: 9, 10, 14-17

*O righteous GOD, who searches minds and hearts,
bring to an end the violence of the wicked and make
the righteous secure. My shield is GOD Most High,
who saves the upright in heart...*
*He who is pregnant with evil and conceives trouble
gives birth to disillusionment. He who digs a hole
and scoops it out falls into the pit he has made. The
trouble he causes recoils on himself; his violence
comes down on his own head. I will give thanks to
the LORD because of His righteousness and will
sing praise to the Name of the LORD Most High.*

NIV

A WORD FROM ME: GOD searches the heart and mind of every person. He knows every thought and intent of the heart and the motives behind every action. The LORD is a shield around those who would suffer from the onslaughts of the wicked. He protects those who call upon His Name. As I have said in past comments, the shield of the LORD is like a sleeve around us, it does not just protect our front, but all directions. The shield of the Most High God covers our head, all sides of our body, under us and IN US. He "saves the upright in heart."

The images of the wicked used in this Psalm are very complete and graphic. He uses the image of pregnancy with evil giving birth to disillusionment. He says that the conception is from trouble. He goes on to say that the "trouble he causes recoils on himself; his violence comes down on his own head." I believe that this is part of the work of the shield of the Most High God, it sends back to the evil one what was intended for those who are found in the shelter of GOD. Think of the shield as a back board in tennis. The player hits the ball to the back board and the ball is returned without any skill or effort from the back board. The Shield of the LORD sends back the slinging arrows of the enemy without hurting or harming the shield or the one protected by the shield. It is also true that the force in which the arrows are sent, that same force is in the velocity of the return.

> "I will give thanks to the LORD because of His righteousness and will sing praise to the Name of the LORD Most High."

PSALM 8:1, 2

O LORD, our LORD, how majestic is Your name in all the earth! You have set Your glory above the heavens. From the lips of children and infants You have ordained praise because of Your enemies, to silence the foe and the avenger.

NIV

A WORD FROM ME: When I look at the heavens and behold the glory of the sky and the earth; when I see a flower, a leaf, a blade of grass, the touch of the wind on them. I see magnificence that cannot be reproduced, though many artists have tried. Each wonder that we behold is breathed into being by the most gracious GOD who paints a beautiful picture, unfolds an awesome tapestry of living things. What glory, what beauty, what wonder!!!!

Watch the wide-eyed wonder of a little child as they look at the first drops of snow. Look into the pure eyes of the infant as they form their first smile or see the first twinkling light. Look at that purity and see the praise that is expressed, wonder-filled, awe-struck, praise. Literally, the foe and the avenger of GOD is silenced by this humble purity.

Have we lost our wonder? Well, we can regain that wonder very quickly by changing our focus. Look at your hands, palm up. See the way your hand is formed and think about the design of each finger and how it works. Look at the skin and remember that there are thou sands of tiny cells, all working together in harmony, and tiny blood drops coursing through each vein and artery. Those veins and arteries, all in sequence, with purpose and function.

GOD designed you and said: "Behold, this is very good." So filled with wonder and with great praise, give thanks to GOD, for He is creator of all.

PSALM 9:1-4

I will give thanks to you, LORD, with all my heart; I will tell of all your wonderful deeds. I will be glad and rejoice in you; I will sing the praises of your name, O Most High. My enemies turn back; they stumble and perish before you. For you have upheld my right and my cause, sitting enthroned as the righteous judge.

NIV

A WORD FROM ME: Psalm 22:3 says, "But thou are holy, O thou who inhabits the praises of Israel." To inhabit, means to live in or to dwell in. Therefore, when we praise God we are reaching into the very dwelling of God and we are entering into His court. This reminds me of Psalm 100:4 which says: "Enter into His gates with thanksgiving, and into His courts with praise; be thankful unto Him and bless His name."

When we praise the Lord with all our heart, tell of His

wonders be glad and rejoice, sing praise and worship Him, all our enemies are turned back, they stumble and perish before Him. Why is this so? Because darkness and light cannot inhabit the same room. JESUS is the light and in Him there is no darkness at all. Our enemy is spiritual darkness, praise is pure light. The darkness of circumstances, of the mind and of the heart will be turned back, stumble and perish when the light of JESUS confronts them.

The choice is ours; do we continue to embrace the darkness, or do we begin to praise the LORD for who He is. The result of entering into the dwelling place of God is: that He brings deliverance; He brings health in mind, body and spirit; He brings the hiding place, so the enemy cannot find us; He increases and strengthens faith; He goes to war against the enemy.

Do you want all these good results to be yours?

The good news is that you can have them right now. Let's just praise the LORD with our whole heart and tell of His wonders.

PSALM 10:16-18

The LORD is King for ever and ever; the nations will perish from His land. You hear, O LORD, the desire of the afflicted; You encourage them, and You listen to their cry, defending the fatherless and the oppressed, in order that man, who is of the earth, may terrify no more.

NIV

A WORD FROM ME: What an extraordinary promise for us to embrace!!! The LORD is King for ever and ever. All things created have an end, but the LORD endures forever. He hears us, He listens to us, He encourages us and defends us. What more could we ever ask?

The real question is: How do we give thanks for all that He has done, is doing and will do for us?

I believe that the answer to that question is easy to answer, but requires discipline to live. My answer to the question is:

"LORD, come into my heart, live in me and live through me. This is the only way that I can give You the thanks that You deserve. Let It be so, forever and ever. AMEN"

We can only give Him the thanks that He is due, by the "living sacrifice" of ourselves to Him, and for His use. I often sing this song to Him:

"How can I say thanks, for the things You have done for me? Things so undeserved, that You give to prove Your love for me. The voices of a million angel, cannot express my gratitude."

ANDRAÉ CROUCH

All that I am and ever hope to be, I offer all to Thee.

TO GOD BE THE GLORY FOR THE THINGS HE HAS DONE.

PSALM 11:4, 5

The LORD is in His Holy Temple; the LORD is on His Heavenly Throne. He observes the sons of men; His eyes examine them. The LORD examines the righteous, but the wicked and those who love violence His soul hates.

NIV

A WORD FROM ME: There are three Temples which are exactly alike: the Temple in Heaven, the Temple on earth and the Temple within each person. The LORD is present, by the Holy Spirit, in each and within each He is the same. GOD is not remote or afar off, looking down on the earth, watching people like we might watch the ants. No, GOD is intimately involved in every aspect of every life, responding and reacting to the actions of man. When we hurt and cry to Him for help, He hears and responds. When we are attacked by evil forces, He sees and reacts by defending our cause.

The LORD examines the heart of a person from the Throne of the Temple within us. He sees and hears those actions and thoughts that are righteous, encouraging us to be strong on that path and feeding us wisdom to follow His way. He also sees and hears those actions and thoughts that are wicked. These actions and thoughts He hates and lets us know that He hates them. Violence is the action of wicked thoughts. GOD hates violence.

During the Advent Season, we are encouraged to examine our ways, our thoughts, and our actions. Those things which are clearly not of GOD, we are challenged, by GOD to repent of them and turn to Him. Those things which are clearly of GOD, we are strengthened in our endurance to follow Him. But the choice is ours: we can choose to turn from those things that GOD hates (wickedness and violence) and return to the LORD; or to stay along the path of wrong and suffer, even more, the consequences of wickedness. The LORD has promised that He will destroy the wicked. That means, if we repent, He is faithful and just to forgive us our sins and deliver us from all the ways of the wicked. You see, wickedness, which GOD will destroy, is a spirit, not a person. Evil comes from one source, Satan, and in the fullness of time, he was destroyed and will be destroyed forever.

People belong to GOD and it is His desire that all be saved.

THAT IS WHAT CHRISTMAS IS ALL ABOUT.
GOD CAME DOWN AT CHRISTMAS TO SAY:
"TELL MY PEOPLE THAT I LOVE THEM"

He is repeating those words right now, today, to every heart. GOD is love, and everyone who loves is begotten of GOD and knows Him.

GOD IS LOVE. LOVE CAME TO EARTH TO SAY: I LOVE YOU.

Your Thoughts

PSALM 12:5-8

"Because of the oppression of the weak and the groaning of the needy, I will now arise," says the LORD. "I will protect them from those who malign them." and the words of the LORD are flawless, like silver refined in a furnace of clay, purified seven times. O LORD, you will keep us safe and protect us from such people forever. The wicked freely strut about when what is vile is honored among men.

NIV

A WORD FROM ME: Oh WOW, is this Psalm like a "sword of the Spirit, piercing even to the dividing asunder of soul and spirit; joint and marrow, and is a discerner of the thoughts and intents of the heart" (Hebrews 4:12) This verse from Hebrews, tells us that it is the Word of GOD, living, powerful and sharp. This Psalm is a part of the Word of GOD. I suggest that you read this Psalm in its entirety. It says that the words of the LORD are flawless, like silver refined in a furnace of clay, purified seven times. This furnace of clay is the body/flesh of the writers of the Word of the LORD. This is an explanation to doubters about the authorship of the Holy Scriptures and its infallibility. GOD inspired it, man wrote it down and we are hearers of the word of GOD.

What I would like to focus on is the activity of GOD on behalf of the poor and the needy. GOD hears the cry of the poor and needy who are oppressed by wicked people. Here, I am not just identifying the homeless poor or those struggling to keep their heads above water in difficult times, like we are in right now. I have found that among the very rich, affluent masses that there is poverty of the soul and spirit that is, equal to or greater than the homeless, struggling masses.

GOD does not distinguish by class, like man does, He sees the heart and hears the cry of the heart. When the weak, needy, and those who are maligned cry for help, He says that He will "arise," He will "protect". When the wicked strut about and when what is vile is honored among men, GOD will execute judgement and, at the same time, shelter those who call to Him for help.

The LORD GOD hears the heart, knows the thoughts and intents (motives), He sees if there is any wickedness within and His judgements are righteous.

In this Advent season, we are called to examine our motives for our actions, why do we do what we do when we do it. If there is any vile way within us, confess it to the LORD and He is faithful and just to forgive us our sin and cleanse us from all unrighteousness. The Blood of JESUS bought us back from death. When we confess our unrighteousness, He forgives and forgets forever. May your Advent be a time of restoration to wholeness in the LORD.

PSALM 13:5, 6

But I have trusted in thy mercy; my heart shall rejoice in Thy salvation. I will sing unto the LORD, because He hath dealt bountifully with me.

KJV

THINK ABOUT IT: David had just cried out to the LORD saying, "How long" before the LORD answers the cry of a faithful servant of the LORD; in other words, "Why the delay, LORD? I need answers *now*." David sounds like so many of us who are caught in situations beyond our control. We cry out to the LORD and He waits for the right time to answer. It is not in our time, it is in His time.

While David is waiting, with the words, "How long!" sounding from the voice of His heart, He enters into the Gates of the LORD with praise, rejoicing, thanksgiving, and a confession of trust in the mercy of the LORD. David chooses to enter into the courts of the LORD with praise, and that praise redirects his thoughts toward GOD.

Psalm 13 only has 6 verses, but in those verses we have a direction for our own life and living. When we are in trouble and we cry out to the LORD for help, expect Him to answer in the right time for a perfect result. Trust Him to have all things in His hand, working them together for good, because he loves us and from Him can only come good things. Waiting is hard, unless you change the direction of your thoughts.

David looked to the LORD GOD and began to enter into His presence through the gate of praise. He remembered the bountiful way in which the LORD had dealt with him in the past and he gave an offering and sacrifice of praise to GOD.

What is an offering and a sacrifice of praise? In very simple words, it is choosing to look into the eyes of the LORD your GOD and remember the greatness and mercy flowing from Him. It is to magnify and glorify the LORD in the midst of trouble, choosing to love the LORD rather than grumble over the circumstances.

I am reminded of a word that the LORD gave me when I was recovering from brain surgery, "Every circumstance is an opportunity to magnify and glorify the LORD." When our eye is fixed on the LORD, then the time of waiting for Him to move on your behalf is filled with the power of praise, lifting the soul to the glorious heights of adoration, which is far above the roar of the sea of circumstances.

The LORD GOD is worthy of all praise, for He has done great things for us and Holy is His Name.

PSALM 14:2

The LORD looked down from heaven upon the children of men, to see if there were any that did understand, and seek GOD.

KJV

"Nevertheless, when the Son of Man cometh, shall He find faith on the earth?"

LUKE 18: 8B

JESUS MADE THE STATEMENT, recorded in Luke, at the end of the parable of the unjust Judge, who gave in to the widow who pestered him, just so he could get rid of her. He gave her justice, because of her persistence. When David made the statement concerning the LORD looking for those who understand and seek GOD, he was saying, what is recorded in Luke, "Shall He (the Son of Man), find faith on the earth?" What connection do faith and understanding have with each other? In this case, they are closely linked; faith comes from GOD and understanding also comes from GOD. When we seek GOD, we receive understanding of circumstances and conditions; through faith, we act on those things revealed by GOD to us.

I see a connection between wisdom and understanding; faith and action. People of faith, act out their faith by seeking GOD for wisdom and understanding. This is the reason the prayer and study of the Scripture is so vital. People of faith, pray without ceasing, because they know that truth, wisdom, knowledge, and righteousness come from GOD and not from their own wits. The more we comprehend the fact that GOD is all knowing, all mighty and always present, the more we will lean on Him rather than lean on our own senses.

Proverbs 3:5, 6 says, "Trust in the LORD with all your heart; and lean not unto thine own understanding. In all thy ways acknowledge Him, and He shall direct thy paths." Seek first the Kingdom of GOD and His righteousness, and all things shall be added unto you. We gain understanding and the faith to act on what GOD imparts to us, by seeking GOD, fervently, and persistently. The Holy Scripture is given to us by GOD, so that we will never be without His Word. The problem is, do we read it, study it, and inwardly digest it?

Do you want understanding from GOD for your life? Do you want the wisdom to live each new day with the knowledge that you are fulfilling the plan of GOD for you and for others? Do you want to please GOD? If your answer to these questions is "yes" then "seek ye the LORD while He wills to be found; call upon Him while He is near." Seek the LORD with all your heart and keep on seeking for the rest of your earthly life. When we shall see Him face to face, we will know all things for ever, because we will know Him in all His glory. We are able to know Him right now; seek Him earnestly.

Your Thoughts:

PSALM 15:1

LORD, who shall abide in Thy tabernacle? Who shall dwell in Thy Holy Hill?

KJV

THINK ABOUT IT: Who? The answer is throughout the Scripture; from Genesis through the Revelation. Who shall dwell in the Holy Hill of GOD forever and ever?

The Psalmist says this: 1. Those who walk uprightly and work righteousness; 2. Those who speak the truth in his heart; 3. Those who do not speak evil against their neighbor; 4. Those who honor and fear the LORD; 5. Those who use their money to feed the poor, without exploiting them. I Corinthians 13 says that faith in the LORD, hope in Him and Love abide, but the greatest of these is love. GOD is Love and everyone who loves is born of GOD and knows Him.

Is it what we do, that gets us to abide in the tabernacle and dwell in the Holy Hill? Or is it what JESUS did on our behalf?

All our efforts to please GOD fall very short of the glory of GOD; we cannot earn our way to heaven. We have been bought with a price, the price of the life of the Only Begotten Son of GOD, JESUS the Christ. He is the door through which we enter into the Presence of the Living GOD.

Then what about the 5 works which please GOD, listed in this Psalm? What about the Ten Commandments? What about all the work of righteousness listed throughout the Scripture? The answer to these questions is found in Deuteronomy 6: 5, "And thou shalt love the LORD thy GOD with all thine heart, and with all thy soul, and with all thy might." All good work is done by GOD through people whom He has chosen and anointed . Therefore, to Him be the glory, the honor and the praise. The Scripture says, "Every good gift and every perfect gift is from above and cometh down from the Father of lights, with whom there is no variableness, neither shadow of turning." (James 1:17) We could also say that every good deed is from the Father and "we are earthen vessels" (2 Corinthians 4:7), crafted for the use of the Master. Therefore, we are servants of GOD, who perform the work He has designed for us to do.

Who shall abide in the tabernacle? Those who worship the LORD from a heart of love for Him and all He created. Who shall dwell in the Holy Hill? Those who believe in the LORD JESUS Christ and are washed in the Blood of JESUS, transformed into His likeness and image.

Think about this: The born-again believer is part of the Blood line of JESUS and heir to His eternal Kingdom. Not by the will of any person, but by the will of Almighty GOD.

PSALM 16:7-9

I will praise the LORD, who counsels me; even at night my heart instructs me. I have set the LORD always before me. Because He is at my right hand, I will not be shaken.

NIV

A WORD FROM ME: We all look for answers to our questions. We are like the little child who is always asking the parent, "Why? Daddy!!!" "Why? Mommy!!!" When we try to answer the endless questions, it only leads to more "Why?" Until we say, in frustration, "Because I said so!".

GOD knows our questions before we even ask. In the silence of the night, when all is still, He counsels us and instructs us. He does this when we "set the LORD always before our eyes". It is a fact that when we are in a "twit," we cannot listen; when we don't listen, we can't hear. The LORD speaks to the heart; this is why JESUS said, "Let not your heart be troubled." A troubled heart cannot hear the voice of the LORD as He counsels and instructs.

There is a saying that I like to use: "I am stirred; but not shaken". We will be stirred by many things. Many trials of our faith will stir us. This is the time when we need to see and hear, with the eyes of faith, the LORD "at my right hand". We are never without Him; we do not stand alone to face the storms of life. He is at our right hand, so that we will not be shaken.

Seek the LORD in the silence of your heart; call upon Him for He is at your right hand. Listen in silence to his instruction and counsel, then arise and shake off the shroud and act on what He has said to your heart. He will give to you a garment of praise for the spirit of heaviness; oil of joy for mourning; and beauty for ashes; that you will become like a tree that bears its fruit and leaves that do not wither. You will be like a watered garden; the planting of the LORD THAT HE MIGHT BE GLORIFIED

PSALM 16:11

Thou wilt show me the path of life. In Thy presence is fullness of joy; at Thy right hand there are pleasures for evermore.

KJV

JESUS SAID, I AM the Way, the Truth and the Life; no man cometh unto the Father but by Me. In Psalm 16: 11, David prays for the coming of the One who would show him the path of life; the One came in the form of the Son of GOD, JESUS the Messiah. The prayer of David was answered in the fullness of time.

There is more prophecy in this verse, in the following words of David, when He said, "In Thy presence is fullness of joy". JESUS was present in the flesh, and there was fullness of Joy. Now, by the Holy Spirit, JESUS is present to us all, and there is fullness of joy. JESUS chose to make His home in each of us, dwelling in our heart. JESUS chose to have us dwell in Him and He holds us in His Heart. (John 17: 23)

David also testifies in Psalm 16: 11 that, "at Thy Right Hand there are pleasures for evermore." This is a prophecy of the ascension of JESUS to sit at the Right Hand of GOD making intercession for us. The Right Hand of GOD is the Hand of power; the Hand of grace and mercy. JESUS sits at the Right Hand of the Father, giving grace, mercy and pleasure to all who believe in Him.

JESUS is the path of Life; JESUS is the Truth concerning all things; and JESUS is the Life of joy and pleasure for evermore. He is the Eternal GOD who is the One Who reconciled man with GOD. Literally, He is the Way to the Father.

This Holy path is open to all who come to Him, and through Him find life and peace. The Love of GOD is unconditionally shone abroad; He reaches out His Hand in compassion to everyone. "As many as receive Him, to them gave He the power to become the Children of GOD, even to them that believe on His name; who were born, not of blood, nor the will of the flesh, nor the will of man, but of GOD." (John 1: 12, 13) It is our choice as to whether we receive Him or reject so wonderful a gift. The gift is freely given, even though it cost the Father the flesh life of His Only Begotten Son. JESUS willingly gave Himself as an offering and sacrifice to GOD for us; all we have to do is receive Him into our Heart.

PSALM 17:8, 9

Keep me as the apple of Your eye; hide me in the shadow of Your wings from the wicked who assail me, from my mortal enemies who surround me.

NIV

A WORD FROM ME: These verses from Psalm 17 remind me of Psalm 91:4: He shall cover thee with His feathers, and under his wings shalt thou trust; His truth shall be thy shield and buckler. These are metaphors for the protection of GOD. He is our "hiding place" our "stronghold," our "fortress", our "deliverer". We stand in the protection of GOD, when we believe in Him and follow Him. There may be storms all around us, enemies trying to hurt or harm us, but the LORD keeps us under the shadow of His wings.

When I think about the wings of GOD, I think about the Prayer Shawl. It has great wings that cover the praying person, so that they are hidden. The shield, I discovered in Psalm 3:3 is like a sleeve which covers from head to toe and all around. The buckler is like the belt of truth in the "Armor of GOD", (Ephesians 6:14) All give the understanding that we are protected and kept safe.

No matter what image you use, when you are surrounded by GOD'S protection, no harm can come near, and no hurt can destroy the Children of GOD. Pastor Randy has given the Congregation a prayer which comes from Job 1:10 - O LORD, build a hedge about me, and about my house, and about all that I have on every side. Bless the work of my hands, and increase my substance in the land. Cause not the wicked to stretch forth their hands to touch me. In JESUS Name, Amen! That hedge is the Blood of JESUS and no evil thing can cross that line.

PSALM 18:1-3

I will love thee, O LORD my strength.
The LORD is my Rock, and my fortress, and my deliverer; my GOD, my strength, in Whom I am will trust; my shield and the horn of my salvation and my high tower.
I will call upon the LORD who is worthy to be praised; so shall I be saved from my enemies.

KJV

THINK ABOUT IT: This Psalm is healed by these words: "A Psalm of David the servant of the LORD, who spoke unto the LORD the words of the song in the day that the LORD delivered him from the hand of all of his enemies, and from the hand of Saul."

It can be said that these are the words you spoke to the LORD on the day that the LORD delivered you from darkness and the power of death. These words explode with the shout of joy like the firecrackers on the 4th of July. They ring out like a thousand Church bells chiming the great Evangel. These words echo through the ages from the heart of all who are born again; leaving the realm of darkness and entering into the glorious light of the glory of GOD. These are the words of the newly Baptized as they come up out of the water, clean from the dirt of sin and clothed in the garment of righteousness. This is the Great Hallel to GOD. Hallelujah, O Lord most high,

David identifies who the LORD is to him: strength, the Rock, fortress, deliverer, GOD in whom he trusts, shield, salvation, high tower, worthy to be praised and Savior. David gives us the picture of JESUS, the Rock the Savior; the Way, the Truth and the Life. He gives us the words to describe our own understanding of the LORD JESUS.

David says, in verse 28, "For Thou wilt light my lamp; the LORD, my GOD, will lighten my darkness." JESUS is the Light and in Him there is no darkness at all. David says, in verse 30, "As for GOD, His way is perfect; the Word of the LORD is proved; He is a shield to all those who trust in Him."

All of Psalm 18 points to JESUS. David says, in verse 46, "The LORD liveth; and blessed be my Rock; and let the GOD of my salvation be exalted."

BE GLORIFIED, JESUS OUR LORD; LET THE WHOLE EARTH SING YOUR PRAISES, FOR YOU ARE THE ROCK OF OUR SALVATION; OUR GOD IN WHOM WE PUT ALL OUR TRUST.

PSALM 19:14

May the words of my mouth and the meditation of my heart be pleasing in Your sight. O LORD, my Rock, and my Redeemer.

NKJV

A WORD FROM ME: I was reading about the heart, from a Biblical understanding, when I came across this definition: "Heart, in Biblical language is the center of the human spirit, from which springs emotions, thoughts, motivations, courage and action — the wellspring of life (Proverbs 4:23)" Proverbs 4: 23 (NIV) says, "Above all else, guard your heart, for it is the wellspring of life." It also says in the Scripture, "Out of the abundance of the heart the mouth speaketh" (Matthew 12:34). These are the words of JESUS concerning the heart and the mouth.

This prayer at the end of Psalm 19 should cause us all to examine our thoughts, to see what our heart is saying before we speak forth words. Words create, just like the words GOD spoke, "Let there be light, and there was light." Our words speak into existence things, the choice for us is: "What things are we creating by our words?" Do we create good or evil? Do we lift up or pull down? Do we encourage or discourage? The choice is ours. The words we speak begin in the heart, so we could also ask, "What is in your heart?" or "What are you meditating on day and night?"

David answers those questions like this: "Thy words have I hidden in my heart, that I might not sin against Thee" (Psalm 119:11) and "Thy word is a lamp unto my feet and a light unto my path" (Psalm 119:105). David calls us to meditate on the Word of GOD day and night, fix our heart on the Holy Word of GOD and then, "Out of the abundance of the heart the mouth will speak" God's word.

I don't think that I am too far from the mark when I say that word spoken apart from GOD'S Word, are vain and idle words, not worth speaking. Words that do not create beauty, wholeness and holiness, should never pass our lips, because they only create ugliness, sickness and sin.

When I lived in Virginia, I was in close association with those who took this very seriously. We would speak the Word of GOD to each other and would build each other up in Holy love. There was no time for idle speaking or vain imaginations, we had our minds fixed on the Scripture. We would say to each other, "Let the words of my mouth and the meditation of my heart be acceptable in Thy sight, O LORD, my Rock and my Redeemer; my strength and my salvation."

PSALM 20

FOR THE PEOPLE OF JAPAN IN THEIR TIME OF GREAT NEED

> *May the LORD answer you when you are in distress;*
> *may the name of the GOD of Jacob protect you.*
> *May he send you help from the sanctuary and*
> *grant you support from Zion. May he remember all*
> *your sacrifices and accept your burnt offerings.*
> *May he give you the desire of your heart and make*
> *all your plans succeed.*
> *May we shout for joy over your victory and lift up our*
> *banners in the name of our GOD. May*
> *the LORD grant all your requests.*
> *Now this I know: The LORD gives victory to his*
> *anointed. He answers him from his heavenly*
> *sanctuary with the victorious power of his right*

> hand. *Some trust in chariots and some in horses, but we trust in the name of the LORD our GOD. They are brought to their knees and fall, but we rise up and stand firm.*
> *LORD, GIVE VICTORY to the king! Answer us when we call!*
>
> NIV

A WORD FROM ME: I want to focus on the translation from the Hebrew. *THE LORD GOD SAVE! *This is what the army of Israel would shout out before battle, "We trust in the Name of the LORD our GOD which we cry out." (Radak) So we cry out to the LORD for the people of Japan, "We trust in the Name of the LORD our GOD. *The LORD GOD SAVE!

Hear our prayer, O LORD, as we cry out to you to save the people of Japan, Haiti, New Zealand, Middle East, and all places where the people are in distress and danger. May the LORD answer you, protect you, and send you help, support you, remember your goodness, and give you the desire of your heart, making all your plans succeed. MAY THE LORD GRANT ALL YOUR REQUESTS.

YOUR THOUGHTS:

PSALM 21:1-4

O LORD, the king rejoices in Your strength. How great is his joy in the victories You give! You have granted him the desire of his heart and have not withheld the request of his lips. You welcomed him with rich blessings and placed a crown of pure gold on his head. He asked You for life, and You gave it to him — length of days, forever and ever.

NIV

A WORD FROM ME: Although this is a Psalm of David, it could be a Psalm coming from our lips. The LORD has won great victories for us. He has shown strength and has granted the desire of our heart and the requests we have made with our lips. The LORD has blessed us richly and has given us the crown of Salvation through JESUS Christ the LORD. We asked for long life and He has given it to us; all His promises are yes and amen. He has provided life Eternal for us, through the willing sacrifice of His only Begotten Son, the atonement. In all ways, we are victorious through Him.

We can join our voices with all the Kings, Prophets, Priests and Apostles who forever sing high praises to GOD for all that He has done for us. We know, as we look into the unknown future, that The LORD GOD reigns over all the earth and He is King of all. In Him is abundant life and through Him we have strength to live well and prosper. Look to Him and be radiant, full of light and joy.

Your Thoughts:

PSALM 22:1, 2; 22-25

My GOD, My GOD, why hast Thou forsaken me? Why art Thou so far from helping me, and from the words of my roaring? O my GOD, I cry in the daytime, but Thou hearest not; and in the night season, and am not silent...

*I will declare Thy name unto my brethren; in the midst of the congregation will I praise Thee. Ye who fear the LORD, praise Him; all ye, the seed of Jacob, glorify Him; and fear him, all ye, the seed of Israel. For He hath not despised nor abhorred the affliction of the afflicted, neither hath He hidden His face from him; but when he cried unto Him, He heard. My praise shall be of Thee in the great congregation; I will pay my vows before them that fear **Him.***

KJV

A WORD FROM ME: "Eli, Eli, lama sabach'thani? My GOD, My GOD, why hast Thou forsaken me?" I have heard these words come from the mouth of many strong people of GOD. Trouble has so gripped them that they can no longer stand; they are in such pain that their mind cannot see any help.

"Where are you, GOD? I cry to you day and night and you don't hear me?" "I am crying to you all the time and I am not silent; I can't be silent, I am in such pain and distress!" JESUS cried like this when He hung on the cross.

His human flesh was crying out in pain, abandonment, and agony. JESUS knew and knows how it feels to be in this place of torment. JESUS identifies with the agony of those who are hanging on the cross of life circumstances. He knows and He hears with passion.

There is sweet relief from the pain and torment, it is declared in verses 22-25 of this same Psalm. When we declare the Name of the LORD, in the sight of all people; when we praise the LORD in the midst of circumstances, it is a testimony of the wonder working power of GOD. When we pay our vows to the Most High GOD in the midst of trouble, people will see and be strengthened and converted to Christ.

What about the one in trouble? What about the one in pain? Is their sweet relief for them? YES, YES, AND YES!!! There is great relief and great strength for the one who is in trouble and in pain. Hear the lesson of Peter, walking on water: JESUS calls Peter to come to Him; Peter jumps out of the boat and walks on the water; as long as he keeps his eyes on JESUS, Peter is joyous. Suddenly, he looks at the stormy waters, taking his eyes off the LORD, and he sinks. "LORD, help me!" he cries, and the LORD puts out His hand and immediately they are in the boat and the sea calms.

When we praise the LORD and proclaim His Name to all

people, we are lifted above the storm of pain and trouble and we walk on the storm as though it was a solid pathway; when we take our eyes off of the LORD, we sink into the storm. JESUS is still with us, we just have taken our eyes off of Him. There is a saying, which I will paraphrase: If you think that GOD has left you, WHO MOVED? Don't move away from the eye to eye contact with the Living LORD.

Your Thoughts:

PSALM 23:4

Yea, though I walk through the valley of the shadow of death, I will fear no evil; for Thou art with me; Thy rod and Thy staff they comfort me.

KJV

A WORD FROM ME: I am late in sending the WORD FROM THE WORD due to recovering from surgery for a broken wrist, right hand, of course. I am writing this WORD with my left hand. While I have been recovering, the LORD has shown me a few things; one of which is about this verse from Psalm 23 and I want to share them with you.

The words "walk through," I have always run past as I said this Psalm by memory. These words carry great meaning. I used to be a runner, one day I hurt my foot so I had to walk. While I was walking along my familiar running route, I noticed things that I had missed, because I was running too fast. There were flowers growing in the grass, houses with beautiful porches, a fence with lovely designs, all of which were new to me, because I was walking slowly.

Since there is no death for those who are born again, because of the resurrection of JESUS, we "walk through the valley of the shad ow of death". We are given the wonderful opportunity to look around and see what we have missed while we were running down the path of life. The rod of correction is there to reveal those things that we have neglected in our Spiritual life and in our care of others. We see the excuses that we make for not doing what the LORD has shown us needed to be done. It is a time to repent and change. The staff is for leaning and balance. The LORD'S staff shows us how to lean on His Word and live a balanced life for Him. It is a time to get the life in order and in focus. There are other things in this valley which are revealed when you "walk"; precious people who really care, tender offerings of comfort, cards, calls, and care. While you are running, you miss the LORD ARISING WITH HEALING IN HIS WINGS. The LORD is always present to us, but we are not always present to Him. He is always near, showing Himself in little gifts of love, just for you to enjoy and be blessed.

John 8: 12 JESUS SAID, "I AM the light of the world; he that followeth me shall not walk in darkness, but have the light of life." The LORD calls us to walk out our life in Him, with our eye on Him always.

PSALM 24:6-10

This is the generation of them who seek Him, who seek Thy face, O Jacob. Lift up your heads, O ye gates; and be ye lifted up, ye everlasting doors; and the King of glory shall come in. Who is this King of glory? The LORD strong and mighty, the LORD mighty in battle. Lift up your heads, O ye gates; even lift them up, ye everlasting doors; and the King of glory shall come in. Who is this King of glory? The LORD of hosts, He is the King of glory.

KJV

A WORD FROM ME: This is the generation who seeks the face of the LORD. I know, there are many who are turning away to seek after their own way of living, but soon they will find out the folly of doing so, and will turn back to GOD. The harvest is plenteous and we need all the laborers to go to the fields. Souls are crying out for help and we are the hands and feet of Christ who bring Eternal help and hope. This commitment is forever and our primary focus. There is no time for part-time Christians, we all have a job to do.

This Psalm is the third of the Messianic Psalms: Psalm 22, depicts JESUS as the Good Shepherd who gives His life for the flock of GOD; Psalm 23 depicts JESUS as the Great Shepherd who watches, guards and keeps the flock of GOD, pasturing each and providing for each individual sheep; Psalm 24 depicts JESUS as the Chief Shepherd who will come again as the strong and mighty LORD of hosts.

I believe that the Everlasting Doors are open in the Spirit. Time is drawing near for the King of glory to come in. I want to remind you that JESUS is also the Door of the Sheepfold (John 10:9) and by Him we are saved and go in and out and find pasture and life.

The Revelation 3: 20 says: "Behold, I stand at the door, and knock; if any man hear my voice, and open the door, I will come in to him, and will sup with him, and he with Me."

LOOK UP, YOUR REDEMPTION DRAWS NEAR.

PSALM 25:1, 2

To you, O LORD, I lift up my soul; in you I trust, O my GOD. Do not let me be put to shame, not let my enemies triumph over me.

KJV

A WORD FROM ME: When David says, "I lift up my soul," he is releasing himself to the sovereignty and protection of GOD. I find this to be a very strong weapon against the power of the enemy of our soul, Satan. When we are in the Hand of GOD, we are hidden from the enemy, we are not seen, because GOD has hidden us "under the shadow of his wings." This release of our self to GOD is a sign of faith and great trust. We will not turn everything we have or will have over to a person in whom we have doubts. GOD is ever faithful, true and creator of all. In Him, alone, can we put our whole being and know that we are safe. JESUS said: "Father, into to Thy Hands I commit my Spirit" His trust in the Father was total, and so should ours.

David asks GOD not to put him to shame. This is not a petition for himself alone, but for all those who depend on him and depend on his faith in GOD to deliver them. David prays for others, that they would not be caused to doubt their faith in GOD.

Who are the enemies? Those enemies of the body are easy to see and when you see them, you know how to protect yourself. Enemies of the soul and the spirit are not as easy to see and not easy to defend against. The Word of the LORD is clear about the enemies of soul and spirit, but which one is attacking and with what weapon in his hand. This is where David gives us a clue about the defense of soul and spirit. Hide in the shadow of the almighty; release your soul and spirit to GOD, because the more of you that is abiding in the shelter of GOD; the less that the enemy can find.

JESUS' Blood is the hedge of protection around us; His Blood covers us and shields us. "By His Blood He reconciled us; by His wounds we are healed." "In Him we live and move and have our being". JESUS IS LORD.

PSALM 26:2,3,8,12

Test me, o Lord and try me,
Examine my heart and my mind;
For your love is ever before me,
I walk continually in your truth....
My feet stand in level ground;
In the great assembly I will praise the Lord.

NIV

A WORD FROM ME: This Psalm reminds me to keep my heart and mind fixed on the Lord. To walk continually in His way of Love and truth.

It is a discipline that engages every past of me. I am so easily distracted by the things of the world, that I can be pulled away from my focus on the Lord and His love. David was in this way with all the things that needs his attention. A thousand things pull me away also.

What brings me back to the reality of the love of God being

ever before me, is the fact that all things come from God and all things and all that we do are done in the sight of God and all His glory.

When I am in the attitude of knowing that God is always present then my feet stand on level ground and from my heart, I can praise Him.

> *"My heart is fixed on God, my heart is fixed, I will sing and give Praise."*
>
> PSALM 57:7 KJV

Your Thoughts:

PSALM 27:1; 13, 14

*The LORD is my light and my salvation whom shall I
  fear? The LORD is the stronghold of my life of
  whom shall I be afraid?*
*I am still confident of this: I will see the goodness of the
  LORD in the land of the living. Wait for the
  LORD; be strong and take heart and wait for the
  LORD. (NIV)*
*I had fainted, unless I had believed to see the goodness
  of the LORD in the land of the living.*

KJV

A WORD FROM ME: As I sat listening to the glorious Easter Service, the first verse of this Psalm came to me, over and over again. "The LORD is my light and my salvation" rings so clear in the Easter Story of the glorious resurrection of JESUS from the darkness of the tomb. JESUS, the Light of the World, conquered the darkness of all of life, when He opened the tomb door, by rolling away the stone. Light conquered the darkness and He continues to conquer the darkness of our mind and heart and life. "In Him there is no darkness at all, the night and the day are both alike; the Lamb is the light of the city of GOD." Shine in my heart, LORD JESUS.

Verses 13 and 14 give a very real look at the human condition. The KJV says: "I had fainted, unless I had believed to see the goodness of the LORD in the land of the living." How many times have we said, "I can't take it anymore!" we would have fainted from the stress of the conditions of life, if it were not for the LORD and for His goodness. The NIV says: "I am still confident of this" we are still confident when we believe and know in our heart that GOD is so good and His mercy is everlasting. All we need to do is wait on Him.

JESUS Christ is risen today, He has burst the prison tomb and opened the door to salvation for all of us, who believe on His Name.

He is the resurrection and the life, in Him there is no darkness, and death is swallowed up in victory.

OH, GLORIOUS DAY OF RESURRECTION,

HE IS RISEN, THE LORD IS RISEN INDEED, HALLELUJAH!

PSALM 27:8

When thou saidst, "Seek My Face," my heart said into thee, "Thy face, LORD will I seek".

KJV

A WORD FROM ME: In prayer, we have an intimacy with GOD that can only be described as "face to face". He shares His breath with us and we breathe in the Holiness of GOD. Breath is the Holy Gift from GOD and how we use that breath is our gift to Him. In prayer, the LORD GOD gives us His breath and we breathe back to Him that which is on our breath. This is very deep communion, a communion JESUS invited us into when He said, "Come unto Me... and I will give you rest".

There is an ancient Icon from the 14th century, painted on an Altar Screen in Decani (former Yugoslavia). It depicts the Virgin Mary holding the infant JESUS, they are cheek to cheek and their lips almost touch. Many have called this, "Shared breath". As I looked deep into this very intimate Mother and

Child painting, I saw what "face to face" really means, it means to "share breath" with the Divine.

JESUS meets us in our time of prayer; He holds us to His Face; we breathe in His breath and are changed. Yes, we will never be the same, as we see the things of this world grow strangely dim, in the light of His Glory and Grace. So, "TURN YOUR EYES UPON JESUS, LOOK FULL IN HIS WONDERFUL FACE."

Your Thoughts:

PSALM 28:6-9

Blessed be the LORD, because He hath heard the voice of my supplications. The LORD is my strength and my shield; my heart trusted in Him, and I am helped. Therefore, my heart greatly rejoiceth, and with my song will I praise Him. The LORD is their strength, and He is the saving strength of His anointed. Save Thy people, and bless thine inheritance; feed them also, and lift them up forever.

BLESS THE LORD AT ALL TIMES, HIS PRAISE CONTINUALLY BE IN YOU MOUTH.

KJV

A WORD FROM ME: Often times, I read the Psalms and miss vital points; this Psalm is one of those. What I missed was the very powerful process of praising GOD before you see the manifestation from His Mighty Hand. THIS IS THE PRAYER OF FAITH.

As the Psalm begins, David is crying out to the LORD for help in his time of need. He is surrounded by evil doers who are not to be trusted. In verse 3 he says, "Draw me not away with the wicked, and with the workers of iniquity, who speak peace to their neighbors, but mischief is in their hearts." He is beset by manipulators and liars who spin words to get their wicked ways accomplished. They are twisters of the truth and distorters of wisdom for their own good. David wants the LORD to deliver him from them and to keep him close to the LORD.

Here is what I missed. He Blesses the LORD, before he sees the manifestation of his answered prayer. He knows the LORD has heard him, by faith in the LORD. He knows that the LORD will act, because of his faith and the history he has with the LORD. In the past, the LORD has done great things for him, because of the great love of the LORD for His people. David knows that the right Hand of the LORD is mighty and will save. So, David confesses this faith in the LORD before he sees the action of the LORD. Literally, if the LORD tarries, David will wait in perfect trust, because he knows the LORD.

My question is, do we know the LORD so well, that we will pray and then thank Him in advance for His action? Do we wait and watch for Him to arise, expecting to see His answer to our prayers? When we pray, do we thank Him that He has heard the voice of our supplication and will answer?

THE PRAYER OF FAITH MOVES MOUNTAINS, OPENS PRISON DOORS, SETS CAPTIVES FREE, BREAKS EVERY YOKE, HEALS HEARTS AND GIVES US A SONG IN OUR HEART TO THE LORD. LET'S SING TOGETHER!!!

I will say with David, "Save Thy people, and bless thine inheritance; feed them also, and lift them up forever."

PSALM 29:10, 11

The LORD sitteth upon the flood: yea, the LORD sitteth King forever. The LORD will give strength unto His people; the LORD will bless his people with peace.

KJV

THE VOICE OF THE LORD

A WORD FROM ME: I did not copy down the words to this entire Psalm, because I want to ask you to read it. In this Psalm there are at least seven references to the VOICE OF THE LORD. Many people ask to hear the voice of GOD, as I read this Psalm, I wonder why a person cannot hear Him? Have we become deaf to the sound of the voice of GOD? How can we recover those ears that hear His voice?

*The Voice of the LORD is upon the waters. The GOD
of glory thunders; the LORD is upon many waters.*
The voice of the LORD is powerful.
The voice of the LORD is full of majesty.
*The voice of the LORD breaketh the cedars; yea, the
LORD breaketh the cedars of Lebanon.*
The voice of the LORD divideth the flames of fire.
*The voice of the LORD shaketh the wilderness; the
LORD shaketh the wilderness of Kadesh*
*The voice of the LORD maketh the hinds to calve, and
strippeth bare the forests; and in His temple doth
everyone speak of His glory.*

KJV

Listen, O my dear friends,
the Voice of the LORD is speaking to
YOU.

PSALM 30:2-5

O LORD, my GOD, I cried unto thee, and Thou hast healed me. O LORD, Thou hast brought up my soul from Sheol; Thou hast kept me alive, that I should not go down to the pit. Sing unto the LORD, O ye saints of His, and give thanks at the remembrance of His Holiness. For His anger endureth but a moment; in His favor is life. Weeping may endure for a night, but joy cometh in the morning.

KJV

A WORD FROM ME: Psalm 30 is a Psalm and song at the dedication of the House of David. It is a song that we can sing as we dedicate our Spiritual House to the LORD. Verses two and three are a statement of the salvation of the soul. When we cry unto the LORD, He hears us and saves us from destruction; He saves our soul from the pit and rescues us from the snare of the enemy. It is a statement of the Redemption brought about by the willing Sacrifice of JESUS.

David prophesied this Redemption; He saw the mighty Hand of GOD and believed GOD for His salvation. David did not realize the total scope of this Salvation, at the time that he prayed and sang this Psalm; he, too, waited for the time of the Atonement by the Blood of JESUS. The Holy Spirit was speaking through David and David burst forth with joyous singing.

We are living in the time of the fulfilled prophecy, so the words of verses four and five should be our song. "Sing unto the LORD, O ye saints of His, and give thanks at the remembrance of His Holiness." JESUS is LORD and He has done great things for us, Holy is His Name. "In His favor is life," through the shed Blood of JESUS and by the Holy Spirit, whom JESUS sent, we live and move and have our being. There is no life apart from JESUS; He is the One who bridged the gap be tween GOD and man. He opened the way for us to be in the presence of the Living GOD forever.

Morning has broken; the weeping of the night has turned to joy and gladness at the rising of the Son in our life. Healing/salvation (the same Greek word — sozo) is ours through JESUS Christ, the One True and Living GOD; By Him, with Him and through Him we live.

PSALM 31:5, 23, 24

Into Thine hand I commit my spirit; Thou hast redeemed me, O LORD GOD of truth... Oh, love the LORD, all ye His saints; for the LORD preserveth the faithful, and plentifully rewardeth the proud doer. Be of good courage, and He shall strengthen your heart, all ye that hope in the LORD.

KJV

A WORD FROM ME: The first words in verse five are the words of JESUS from the cross. JESUS released His Spirit to His Father and literally, gave back the breath that the Father had given Him. Notice what I said about "breath," "He gave back the breath that the Father had given Him." We have all been given the breath of life, so that we can live; when this breath is taken away, we cannot live, move and have our being. It is GOD who gives us the gift of breath. Notice what is said in Genesis 2:7

and in Psalm 104: 29, 30. It could be said that we have the stewardship of the breath GOD has given us. So, "Don't waste your breath."

In these words from verse 5, we also see another fact; JESUS, David and we show trust, by releasing our spirit to GOD. David says: "Thou hast redeemed me, O LORD GOD of truth," this is a statement of trust in the one who is perfect truth. Daily, I find myself releasing my life to GOD with these words of verse 5. I release my life, my day and my breath to GOD, because He is the only one who is perfect truth and trustworthy.

My prayer for all of us is reflected in verses 23, 24. "Oh, love the LORD, all ye His saints; for the LORD preserveth the faithful, and plentifully rewardeth the proud doer. Be of good courage, and He shall strengthen your heart, all ye that hope in the LORD." AMEN.

Your Thoughts:

PSALM 32:6-8, 11

Therefore let everyone who is godly pray to You while You may be found; surely when the mighty waters rise, they will not reach him. You are my hiding place; You will protect me from trouble and surround me with songs of deliverance. "I will instruct you and teach you in the way you should go; I will counsel you and watch over you"....
Rejoice in the LORD and be glad, you righteous; sing, all you who are upright in heart.

REJOICE IN THE LORD ALWAYS, AND AGAIN I SAY REJOICE

A WORD FROM ME: Those words, "You are my hiding place" are so strong and create such peace to a troubled soul. Corrie Ten Boom wrote a whole book on her time in a concentration camp during the Nazi Holocaust, entitled "The Hiding Place". What she found and many others have born witness that the LORD GOD shelters, hides, covers, and renders invisible, those who run to Him for help in the time of need. Is this hiding place only available during the time of need and distress, or is it like a closet, where we can go and shut the door?

In Matthew 6:6 JESUS says, "But thou, when thou prayest, enter into thy closet and shut thy door, pray to thy Father, who is in secret; and thy Father, who seeth in secret, shall reward thee openly." This tells me that the hiding place is the closet of prayer to the Father and the "door" is praise of the Living GOD. JESUS says the He is the door. This also tells me that I am called to enter into this hiding place of prayer often, daily, moment by moment, or as

Paul says, "Without ceasing". When we are in prayer, in the closet within our spirit, we are hidden from the enemy and the "mighty waters that rise". We are sheltered by the almighty, sovereign GOD. He will instruct us, He will guide us in the way we should go; He will guide us with His eye. There are no questions that He cannot answer; He will answer; we must go into the closet and shut the door and LISTEN .

Instead of worry about circumstances which arise like the mighty waters and threaten to drown the soul, we can run into the hiding place of the Most High GOD and rise above the storm on the wings of praise.

PSALM 33:1-4, 6

Rejoice in the LORD, O ye righteous; for praise is befitting to the upright. Praise the LORD with the harp; sing unto Him with the psaltery and an instrument of ten strings. Sing unto Him a new song; play skillfully with a loud noise. For the word of the LORD is right, and all His works are done in truth... By the word of the LORD were the heavens made, and all the hosts of them by the breath of His mouth.

KJV

A WORD FROM ME: Praise pleases GOD; praise glorifies GOD; praise brings increase; praise saves from the enemy and brings deliverance; praise brings the presence of GOD; praise brings healing; praise brings salvation; the power of praise is enormous, lifting all those who love the LORD into His presence where there is life and breath. Praise from the heart dispels all the darkness and gloom of circumstances, lifting us up on wings and clothing us with the garment of praise.

Praise is powerful, it acknowledges that the LORD is good; the LORD is mighty; the LORD is faithful; the LORD is King and the earth rejoices. In His presence is fullness of joy and at His right Hand are pleasures forever more. Praise eliminates doubt and strengthens faith. So let us sing, play, shout, dance and proclaim that "JESUS CHRIST IS LORD, TO THE GLORY OF GOD THE FATHER."

The Word of the LORD has gone forth and the earth was created; He saw each of us and spoke us into being; He gave us His breath and we live; He called us by name and we are His chosen people. "The eye of the LORD is upon those who fear Him, upon those who hope in His mercy." (Psalm 33: 18)

> Let everything that hath breath, praise the LORD;
> Praise ye the LORD.

PSALM 33:12, 13; 18

Blessed is the Nation whose GOD is the LORD; and the people whom He hath chosen for His own inheritance. The LORD looketh from heaven; He beholdeth all the sons of men... Behold, the eye of the LORD is upon those who fear Him, upon those who hope in His mercy.

KJV

A WORD FROM ME: This week we will celebrate the birth of our Nation. The United States of America is a land flowing with milk and honey, because the LORD has blessed her. The eye of the LORD has looked with favor on this land; we have blessed the LORD and He has blessed us.

The United States of America has stood with Israel, our elder brother in the LORD; A Nation to whom GOD declared His Name and gave his Covenant. Out of Israel the Father nurtured His Son, en trusting Him to the care of the People of

GOD. The United States of America stands today with Israel, our brother and our friend.

GOD beholds and watches over us; the eye of the LORD is upon them who fear Him and hope in His mercy. GOD never slumbers or sleeps; He watches and responds with great love. The Nation of GOD are those who embrace the LORD with their whole heart, found throughout the world; from Him flows all grace, mercy and love, like a fountain of living water in a dry and thirsty land.

The LORD GOD gave His highest and His best for the salvation of humankind. He asks nothing in return except that we love and serve Him. We, who love Him, form the nation whose GOD is the LORD and the people whom He has chosen for his inheritance.

Let us arise, people of GOD, and STAND together, arm in arm, shoulder to shoulder, in full armor of GOD; a mighty force that is called and blessed by the LORD.

PSALM 34:8, 9; 11; 19, 20

Taste and see that the LORD is good; blessed is the man who takes refuge in Him. Fear the LORD, you His saints, for those who fear Him lack nothing... Come, my children, listen to me; I will teach you the fear of the LORD... A righteous man may have many troubles, but the LORD delivers Him from them all; He protects all His bones, not one of them will be broken.

NIV

THE FEAR OF THE LORD IS THE BEGINNING OF WISDOM

A WORD FROM ME: This Psalm is filled with many good things for us to hear from the LORD. We need to listen to HIM; we need to believe, in our heart, what He says is true; we need to confess that the LORD will stand by His promises and will do what He says.

The fear of the LORD is to know Him, follow Him, extol Him, and Love Him; without limits. Some of us put limits on our praise of GOD. We either praise Him in good times, because we are feeling good; or we praise Him in bad times, because we want deliverance from our troubles. I want to suggest that there should be no limits to our love, praise, exalting of the LORD. He has no limits to HIS goodness towards us; we should have no limits to our honoring of HIM.

In this life, we all will have troubles; we may feel that the very structure of our life is going to break apart (bones is a word that means structure, skeletal structure). Verses 19 and 20 speak to this, I will paraphrase, Those who are rightly related to GOD through honor and praise of HIM will have troubles from time to time, but the LORD will deliver him/her from all of them; HE protects the very skeletal structure of our life so that it will not be broken, not even a piece of it will fall off. (These are my words.)

If you want an example of how the LORD GOD protects the bones of His righteous ones, look at JESUS on the cross, not one of HIS bones was broken and the skeletal structure of HIS life remained intact through the death of HIS body, the Resurrection from the dead and HIS ascension to the right hand of the Father. HIS Spiritual skeletal structure remains whole forever and ever. This is so for us, also, who believe on HIS Name and live in HIM, for where HE is, and there we shall be also.

PSALM 35:27, 28

May those who delight in my vindication shout for joy and gladness; may they always say, "The LORD be exalted, who delights in the well-being of His servants." My tongue will speak of Your righteousness and of Your praises all day long.

NIV

A WORD FROM ME: It is believed that this Psalm was written during the time that Saul was chasing David to kill him. David was in fear of his life, due to the anger of King Saul. The whole Psalm is filled with this kind of haunted speech, except for the final lines which are quoted here. We get a glimpse of the great love David has for the LORD and his desire for the LORD to be glorified, by him and by others.

We can learn a real lesson from David; when life gets really tough, and even our life is threatened by circumstances; we should stop our journey down the road of complaining and turn our feet to the road of praising the LORD. Most of us can relate to the first 26 verses of this psalm, but we should take careful notice of the last two verses, which turn the whole focus to the LORD.

"My tongue will speak of Your righteousness and of Your praises all day long" should be our heart cry even in the midst of horror and unfair persecution. Praise lifts the circumstances from the muck and mire and places them in the Hands of GOD. In His Hands all circumstances are healed, restored and made completely whole.

Your Thoughts:

PSALM 36:8-10

For with thee is the Foundation of Life; in Thy light shall we see the Light. Oh, continue Thy lovingkindness unto those that know Thee, and Thy righteousness to the upright in heart.

KJV

A WORD FROM ME: In the LORD GOD is a foundation of life. JESUS said to the woman at the well: "If thou knowest the gift of GOD and Who is that saith to thee 'Give me to drink' thou wouldst have asked of Him, and He would have given thee Living Water." (John 4:10)

JESUS in the Living Water, the foundation of Life. When we drink of the water of Life, it becomes a fountain springing up to Eternal Life. (John 4:14)

JESUS is the light that lightens our path (Psalms 119:105). We will never walk in darkness when the Light of the Word of GOD goes before us.

The sign of the Water of Life and the Light of the Word shining through a soul, is the abundance of Loving Kindness and Righteousness pouring forth from the heart

O, continue to pour forth the Water of Life through us.

Your Thoughts:

PSALM 37:10, 11

Yet a little while, and the wicked shall not be; yea, thou shalt diligently consider his place, and it shall not be. But the meek shall inherit the earth, and shall delight themselves in the abundance of peace.

KJV

A WORD FROM ME: "Yet a little while..." is a word of hope for those in the middle of a struggle. While the storm is raging, and the waves of circumstances seem to be so overwhelming that they threaten to capsize your whole world, it is hard to think that there will be an end. The little word, "Yet a little while…" can be of great comfort. We can endure most anything, if we know that it won't last long, but when you are in the middle of the fire it is hard to see that the end is near. You have to see with the eyes of faith.

Have you had a terrible headache that you thought would never go away? Have you said, "I can't stand it anymore?" Have you experienced the headache go away; you look for it and it is gone? Have you felt the sweet relief? This is what trouble, torment, troublemakers and wicked people are like. They are like a fierce headache or heart ache that seems to never go away. But, in the fullness of the LORD'S time, He will remove the trouble, torment, troublemaker and the wicked. You will look for them and they will be gone; you will hunt for them and their place in this world will be no more. GOD has removed them. The meek, those who are teachable and humble, will inherit the earth and delight themselves in the abundance of peace. JESUS spoke about this in the Beatitudes, quoted by Him in Matthew 5:5.

The meek will inherit the earth, because they trust in the sovereignty of GOD and will obey His will, without question. The key to overcoming the torment of circumstances beyond our control is to submit to the authority of the LORD. Humble yourself in the sight of the LORD and He will lift you up. The torment will be no more; you will look for it and not find it. You will rest in peace. Be meek, teachable and humble and submit to the will of GOD, trusting in His sovereignty.

PSALM 38:21, 22

Forsake me not, O LORD, O my GOD, be not far from me. Make haste to help me, O LORD, my salvation.

KJV

A WORD FROM ME: Psalm 38 is a Psalm of sorrow for sin. David expresses the heart wrenching cry of his heart for forgiveness from a terrible conviction of sin. He says in verses 17, and 18, "For I am ready to halt, and my sorrow is continually before me. For I will declare mine iniquity; I will be sorry for my sin."

These are the words of a heart that is ready for conversion; ready to be saved and set free from the bond age of sin. It is also a statement of faith in the LORD; a knowledge that "if you confess your sin, He is faithful and just to forgive you your sin and cleanse you from all unrighteousness" I know, this is a New Testament understanding - 1 John 1: 9 - but, this understanding was very much alive in the heart of David and expressed vividly in this Psalm. The LORD gave him the way to walk in righteousness.

David says that he is "ready to halt," verse 17, he is ready to stop the way of sin in his life; he is ready for redemption. How many of us have reached this place in our life and we said, "I am ready to halt?" When we are "ready to halt" the LORD JESUS is ready to cleanse and redeem. It is by His Blood that we have the cleansing of our sin, no matter how notorious. It is by His Blood that we are reconciled to GOD. JESUS is right there, standing before us, ready to hear the words, "I am ready to halt, and my sorrow is continually before me. For I will declare mine iniquity; I will be sorry for my sin." He will then wash away all our sin and cleanse us from all unrighteousness; making us fit to enter into the Courts of the LORD with praise. "What can wash away my sin? Nothing but the Blood of JESUS. What can make me whole again? Nothing but the Blood of JESUS."

There is a new life of perfect freedom ready for all who will confess their sin unto Almighty GOD. If there is the bondage of sin wrapped around you like a great boa constrictor, squeezing the life out of you, say, "I am ready to halt" and declare all iniquity to the LORD. He will "make hast to help" you, for He is the GOD of our Salvation.

PSALM 39:1

I said, I will take heed to my ways, that I sin not with my tongue; I will keep my mouth with a bridle, while the wicked is before me.

KJV

A WORD FROM ME: This reminds me of the many times that JESUS did not speak; he was silent in the face of vile attacks. "Like a sheep before his shearers is dumb, he opened not his mouth." I am reminded also that JESUS only spoke what He heard the Father speak, so, the Father GOD must have been silent also.

Wickedness does not deserve a response; instead, the wicked words must fall to the ground and return to the source of the wickedness, the Devil himself. I have heard this image used often, "Let the words bounce off of your shield and return to sender." Silence is a clear shield and sure defense; after all it is the shield of faith.

If you are like me, you want to return fire and put out the wicked with shattering words. Let me share what I have learned; we must give account for all the words we speak to GOD; and so do they. The wicked need lots of prayer for their words to be forgiven, washed in the Blood of JESUS, and cleansed from all unrighteousness. I learned this lesson by having been attacked viciously, by a wicked mouth. As I stood in silence, I prayed for their forgiveness, that their wicked words would not be held to their charge.

> WE ALL MUST GIVE ACCOUNT TO GOD
> FOR ALL THE WORDS WE SPEAK.

May all of our words be acceptable unto GOD and pleasing to His Heart.

PSALM 40:1-4

I waited patiently for the LORD, and He inclined unto me and heard my cry. He brought me up also out of a horrible pit, out of the miry clay, and set my feet upon a Rock, and established my goings. And He hath put a new song in my mouth, even praise unto our GOD; many shall see it and fear, and shall trust in the LORD. Blessed is the man who maketh the LORD his trust, and respecteth not the proud, nor such as turn aside to lies.

KJV

A WORD FROM ME: Psalm 40 is one of the Messianic Psalms, which foreshadows the mission and ministry of JESUS. I also find in this Psalm great words of encouragement for those of us who live now. When we wait patiently for the LORD, He does many things:

1. He inclines his ear and hears;
2. He brings us out of the pit, which is very deep;
3. He brings us out of the miry clay, which draws us downward;
4. He sets our feet on the Rock. The Rock is JESUS;
5. He establishes our goings, He is the way and the path to walk in;
6. He puts a new song in our mouth which is praise unto GOD;
7. He blesses us; seven acts of GOD for us who wait patiently for Him.

But waiting patiently is not easy when you are in the midst of crisis. When deadlines loom and there seems to be no answer, it is easy to fall into fear and darkness, which is a "miry clay" sucking us down ward. Faith in the mighty power of the LORD and the confession of faith, sets in motion a powerful force that works on our behalf. He sets our feet on solid Rock and establishes our goings. He puts a new song in our mouth, even praise of our GOD.

I want to share with you a little secret, when you thank the LORD, praise Him and exercise your faith before you see the light at the end of the tunnel, you will be lifted up out of the pit and miry clay immediately. Faith in the resurrection power of GOD lifts us up; darkness flees and light dispels the gloom and fear. Fear cannot live with faith. I repeat: FEAR CANNOT LIVE WITH FAITH.

There is another aspect to the gift of waiting patiently for the LORD, many shall see and fear the LORD and trust in Him. They and you will be blessed. Yes, a multitude of people will see the struggle and the manifestation of the LORD; they will witness your patience and turn to the LORD.

Verse 4 sums up the whole scene: "Blessed is the man who maketh the LORD his trust, and respecteth not the proud, nor such as turn aside to lies."In a crisis, it is easy to start "grabbing at straws", looking for any kind of fix to the problem, but this can lead to the pit; trust in the LORD leads to blessing, favor and prosperity. It is for HIS Holy Name Sake that HE works all things together for good; it is out of HIS great Love that HE saves us.

YOUR THOUGHTS:

PSALM 41:1-3

Blessed is he that considereth the poor; the LORD will deliver him in time of trouble. The LORD will preserve him, and keep him alive; and he shall be blessed upon the earth, and thou wilt not deliver him unto the will of the enemies. The LORD will strengthen him upon the bed of languishing, thou wilt make all his bed in his sickness.

KJV

A WORD FROM ME: Whatever does it mean, "thou wilt make all his bed in his sickness"? I pondered this verse and looked it up in many sources. One source says that the LORD will raise the sick up from their bed of sickness. Matthew Henry Commentary says that this is an illustration of how the LORD will work through those who assist the sick, like nurses and attendants. The LORD will "make all his bed from head to foot, so that no part shall be uneasy; he will turn his bed or shake it up and make it easy; or He will turn it into a bed of health... The soul shall, by His grace, be made to dwell at ease when the body lies in pain." Notice who it is that does all this; IT IS THE LORD.

I hear an echo in these verses, "Blessed are the merciful, for they shall obtain mercy" These are the words of JESUS in Matthew 5:7. The LORD notices the kindness given to the poor, sick and needy, He Blesses those who spend their time ministering to them. How does He do this? By delivering them from trouble, preserving them, keeping them alive, blessing them, delivering them from evil (another quote from JESUS, Matthew 6: 13), strengthen and make his bed.

WOW! This should want to make all of us run to help the poor, the sick and the needy.

Here is a watch word: WATCH YOUR MOTIVES.

Is your motive for responding to the poor, because of what you will get from the LORD? Or is your motive compassion and mercy for whoever is in need? The gifts from the LORD are just that, gifts. He knows the heart and the pure heart will receive from His Hand grace in our time of need.

Another Note: WHO IS THE ONE WHO DOES THE WORK?

When we consider the poor and the sick, the LORD does the work of restoring them and keeping them alive. We are only the hands and feet of the LORD. Therefore, to HIM BELONGS THE GLORY, GREAT THINGS HE HAS DONE.

Could it be, that, "considering the poor" is an act of intercession and offering our self for the LORD to move? THINK ABOUT IT!!!!

PSALM 42:1, 2

As the hart panteth after the water brooks, so panteth my soul after thee, O GOD. My soul thirsteth for GOD, for the living GOD; when shall I come and appear before GOD?

KJV

A WORD FROM ME: I live in Arizona where it is dry and hot. The humidity can get to single digits and stay there for weeks and months. Animals, plants, humans and insects all need water for life and water is precious in Arizona. Water is so precious that people fight over it like it was a piece of gold or a precious gem. Phoenix wants the water for its people and water parks for amusement; ranchers and farmers need the water for their crops and animals; people need the water for themselves and their landscapes; firemen need the water to put out wildfires caused by nature or carelessness. Everyone in AZ argues over water and water rights.

The Psalmist is not talking about "water rights" in the human sense; He is talking about his thirst for GOD. The Water of Life is given freely to all who ask for it. The problem lies in the fact that we don't ask for it. Moses was told first to strike the Rock in the wilderness and the water would gush out. He did and it did. Next, he was told to speak to the Rock and the water would gush out; he hit the rock instead. We are still thinking that we need to strike the Rock to get Living Water; there are many who think that they have to yell at the Rock and demand water. There are many who think that they are the only ones entitled to the Water of Life and others have to beg them for a drink. JESUS says, "Come, to the water of life and you who have no money, come, buy and drink."

The water of Life is free to all who ask the LORD. JESUS was struck, bled, died and rose again to open the way to the Water of Life.

JESUS defeated death and is seated with the Father, interceding for us before the Throne of Grace. The Psalmist asks, "When shall I come and appear before GOD?" The answer is RIGHT NOW Are you thirsty for GOD, "Come and drink!" JESUS is right here, all the time, by the Holy Spirit, whom He sent. He is not at a distance, you don't have to beat or yell to get His attention, you don't have to bargain and beg for his time. He is focused on your life and your needs, RIGHT NOW. JESUS opened the door for us to come to the Throne of Grace and have instant access to GOD, through HIM. The Water of Life is free; access to GOD is open; all you have to do is ASK and it will be given to you.

PSALM 42:7, 8

Deep calleth unto deep at the noise of Thy waterspouts; all Thy waves and Thy billows are gone over me. YET the LORD will command His lovingkindness in the daytime, and in the night His song shall be with me, and my prayer unto the GOD of my life.

KJV

A WORD FROM ME: "Deep calleth unto deep at the noise of Thy waterspouts"; there is a noise that circumstances sound. It sounds like the deafening sound of crashing waves on the shore; of the thunder of angry billows against the sea walls. The sound can be so deafening that no one can speak over the noise. Again and again the waves crash and then withdraw, just to crash again. The waves seem to rise from the deepest places of the sea.

Within us, there are three levels — a trinity. There is the body, the soul and the spirit three in one person; one person in three parts. These deep places call to one another with a voice they can understand. When the soul is troubled, it calls to the spirit — "help me, save me, deliver me." At the same time, the soul is calling to the body — "rescue me, do something, I am drowning." The sound of the trinity within can be so loud that your head is only hearing the crash against the sea wall of your mind. It is like being flooded by the waves and billows.

When we live in the "YET THE LORD," we find the lovingkindness of GOD commanding the waves to be still as the Light of Christ brings the daytime in our life. Then in the night season, when darkness again returns to our way, there is a song within, a prayer to the LORD, that silences the sound of the thunder and speaks peace to the body, the soul and the spirit. This "song in the night" unites the trinity of the person into one and the "prayer unto the GOD of my life" unites the body, soul and spirit with the Holy Trinity, Father, Son and Holy Spirit, THE ONE.

I know, and have discovered in my life, that when the crash of dark times deafens the whole being; the "song in the night and the prayer unto the GOD of my life" will speak peace and the storm will obey the voice of the LORD when He says: "PEACE, BE STILL."

PSALM 43:3, 4

Send forth Your light and Your truth, let them guide me; let them bring me to Your holy mountain, to the place where You dwell. Then will I go to the altar of GOD, to GOD, my joy and my delight. I will praise You with the harp, O GOD, my GOD.

TLV

A WORD FROM ME: As I look at these verses, I realize that this prayer of David has already been accomplished. I can come to the "Holy Mountain, to the place where You (GOD) dwell." David prayed that he would be allowed to come and be in the presence of GOD, his joy and delight, so that he could praise the LORD with his harp, sing songs of praise to GOD, his GOD.

Well, his prayer was answered and now we can come every moment of every day to the Holy Mountain and sing songs of praise to GOD. WHEN WAS THIS PRAYER AN SWERED?

WHEN DID THE DOOR OPEN? WHY CAN WE COME ANY TIME TO THE MOUNTAIN OF THE LORD?

David prayed that the LORD would "send for Your light and Your truth." JESUS is the Light and He is the Truth, personified. He came and said: "I Am the Light of the World." and "I AM the way, the Truth and the Life." When JESUS said, "I AM" He was using the Holy Name and declaring that He is GOD. He Is the ONE sent from GOD to open the way to the Mountain of the LORD. Through JESUS we are able to sit with Him, pray with Him, walk with Him and listen to His guidance.

The Light and the Truth guides us and brings us all the way along the path of this earthly life, until we dwell with Him forever in Glory. The sacrifice of GOD, sending His only begotten Son; the precious Blood of JESUS upon the Altar in the Holy Place, opened the door and by the Holy Spirit, sent from GOD, we can come into His glorious presence.

Why don't we come? Why don't we sit? Why don't we listen? Are we so busy doing things and thinking things and listening to strange voices that we have no time for GOD?

I hope that you are struck by that last question. Struck so hard that you drop to your knees with great sorrow for having neglected GOD, pushing Him to the side and saying, "Later GOD, not now, I am too busy for you."

David yearned to be in the Presence of GOD. His yearning was so strong that He cried out to GOD for communion with Him. Let every cell of your being cry out to GOD for His Presence in your everyday life. Spend time with Him in Holy Communion, drink Him in and partake of His life in you. Pray without ceasing; praise Him with out ceasing; glory in Him and meditate on Him in your heart without ceasing.

"Put your hope in GOD, for I will yet praise him, my Savior and my GOD." Psalm 43:5

PSALM 44:23-26

Awake, why sleepest Thou, O LORD? Arise, cast us not off forever.
Wherefore hidest Thou Thy face, and forgettest or affliction and our oppression? For our soul is bowed down to the dust; our belly cleaveth unto the earth. Arise for our help, and redeem us for Thy mercies' sake.

KJV

A WORD FROM ME: "Awake, why sleepest Thou, O LORD?" These words have crossed the lips of most of us at one time or another. "Where are you, LORD?" "Where were you, LORD?" I heard many say ask these questions when the storms hit the East Coast, the Gulf of Mexico, fires in the West and earthquakes. "Arise, why sleepest Thou, O LORD?"

For our answer, I want to turn to the Gospel account of the storm on the lake; Luke 8:22-25. Notice that JESUS fell asleep and there came down a mighty wind. The disciples woke Him and said, "Master, Master, we perish!" When He awoke, He rebuked the wind and it became calm. Verse 25 contains the words of JESUS, "Where is your faith?"

I ask the same question that JESUS asks, "Where is your faith?" Do we have faith in the fatal outcome of conditions? Are we sure that when bad things happen that we are going to perish? OR Is our faith in the LORD, who calms the sea and commands the winds?

OK, you want to know my thoughts on those who have died because of the terrible happenings in their lives; storms, destruction, devastation, ruin and death. Where is your faith, Rebecca?

The LORD JESUS opened the way to Eternal life, THERE IS NO DEATH IN JESUS. He went and prepared the way for all of us to live with Him; those who have died in Him are with Him in glory and are ALIVE.

Where is your faith regarding those who have lost everything and yet are alive? The LORD has promised that He will provide and He does, in miraculous ways. I believe that we, who are not affected by the devastation, are part of the provision of GOD for the needs of those who are suffering. If we can't help directly, we can join JESUS in prayer for those who suffer. Intercession is our call from the LORD. We are to intercede in faith believing that the LORD will do what He has promised. Jeremiah 24: 6, 7 says "For I will set mine eyes upon them for good, and I will bring them again to this land; and I will build them, and not pull them down; and I will plant them, and not pluck them up, and I will give them an heart to know me, that I Am the LORD, and they shall be my people, and I will be their GOD; for they shall return unto Me with their whole heart." OR "For I know the thoughts that I think toward you, saith the

LORD, thoughts of peace, and not of evil, to give you an expected end. Then shall ye call upon me, and ye shall go and pray unto me, and I will hearken unto you. And ye shall seek me, and find me, when ye shall search for me with all your heart. And I will be found by you, saith the LORD." (Jeremiah 29: ll-14a)

The Disciples went to JESUS who was asleep in the boat, which was intercession and prayer. He rebuked the wind and it became calm, which was answered prayer. ARISE, PEOPLE OF GOD AND PRAY IN FAITH, BELIEVING THAT YOU HAVE WHAT HE HAS PROMISED.

PSALM 45:6, 7

Thy throne, O God (Judge, in the Hebrew), is forever and ever; the scepter of thy kingdom is a right scepter. Thou lovest righteousness, and hatest wickedness; therefore GOD, Thy GOD hath anointed thee with the oil of gladness above thy fellows.

KJV

IN ANCIENT TIMES, the King was known as a god, but the Hebrew people would call them judges. The use of the word "judge" helps to clarify this passage. King David was anointed King by GOD and a covenant was made with him that his kingdom would be forever. This became very real with the coming of the Messiah, from the house and lineage of David; who took the Throne of the Everlasting Kingdom in Heaven.

A note from Iban Ezra and cited in Radak is that "Thy Throne, O GOD" refers to GOD and His throne; the only

Throne that is forever and ever. This does not conflict with the other interpretation, since the Jewish people are reluctant to call any mortal man a god, they use Judge instead. GOD, blessed be He, anoints the King; therefore it is the Throne of GOD. JESUS is GOD; therefore He has the Divine Right to the Eternal Throne and He ascended to it and sits on it.

Righteousness is the scepter of His kingdom and he hates wickedness and loves righteousness. What is righteousness? It is the right relationship with GOD. "Therefore GOD, thy GOD hath anointed thee with the oil of gladness above thy fellows." A right relationship with GOD, through the yielding of self to GOD for His use, brings the confidence and competence that establishes joy and stability. We can learn a lot from this verse. What is the "oil of gladness"? It is the anointing of the Holy Spirit, the comforter. "Comfort" is an interesting word, "com-" means with, and "-forte" means strength. Not only does the Holy Spirit give joy and gladness, but He gives strength directly from the Throne of GOD.

One thing that I notice, in this verse, is that righteousness, a right relationship with GOD, brings the authority of GOD into a life, the scepter is the sign of authority. This authority, with the discernment of GOD, gives knowledge of right and wrong. Our choice then becomes whether we hate evil and love righteousness or hate righteousness and love evil. When we choose for GOD to reign in our life, then we have the anointing with the oil of gladness, even in the midst of deep darkness. The choice remains with us; the LORD says, "Choose life," love righteousness.

The next thing that I notice is that, through living our life in right relationship with GOD, we are formed into the likeness of the One who is righteous. This transformation brings with it a joy that is deep, profound, and everlasting.

When you read the whole Psalm, for me, it has the ring of the Marriage Feast of the Lamb in the Revelation (Rev. 21: 1-8). Through out this Psalm, I see JESUS as the mighty king with the scepter of His Kingdom that will be forever and ever. I see the bride, adorned for her husband and all the hosts of Heaven glorifying GOD forever and ever.

PSALM 46:4, 5

There is a river, the streams whereof shall make glad the city of GOD; the holy place of the tabernacle of the Most High. GOD is in the midst of her; she shall not be moved. GOD shall help her and that right early.

KJV

There is a river whose streams make glad the city of God, the holy place where the Most High dwells. God is within her, she will not fall; God will help her at break of day.

NIV

A WORD FROM ME: What is this river? Where is this river? Is the river a body of water or a metaphor for a spiritual fact?

I believe that this river is a stream of living water which flows from the Throne of GOD into the dry and thirsty land of humanity. I believe that this river is actually the Holy Spirit of GOD who dwells within the heart of those who love the LORD. Isaiah spoke of this in these words: "And the LORD shall guide thee continually, and satisfy thy soul in drought, and make fat thy bones; and thou shalt be like a watered garden, and like a spring of water, whose waters fail not." (Isaiah 58: 11 KJV)

Ezekiel says this: "And I will put my Spirit within you, and cause you to walk in my statutes, and ye shall keep mine ordinances, and do them:" And JESUS said, "I in them, and thou in me, that they may be made perfect in one; and that the world may know that thou hast sent me, and hast loved them, as thou hast loved me." (John 17: 23); "But when the Comforter is come, whom I will send unto you from the Father, even the Spirit of truth, who proceedeth from the Father, He shall testify of me; and ye also shall bear witness, because ye have been with me from the beginning." (John 15: 26, 27)

The LORD puts within the believer, the Tabernacle of the Most High, the place of Holy worship. This place is a place of Holy rest and silence in the Presence of the LORD. Here we can sit with JESUS and feast on him in our heart. Here we are fed with Living water, flowing under the Throne of GOD. Here we are nurtured and nourished, taught the wisdom of GOD and are flooded with great love.

How do we get into the river? We get there through prayer, the deep prayer of being overflowed by the river. Read Ezekiel 47 1-12 for the process of entering the river of the Presence of the Holy Spirit. GOD wants us in that river with Him; He is in the midst of the river. He is calling each of us to enter and be washed in His Love.

PSALM 46:10, 11

Be still and know that I AM GOD; I will be exalted among the nations, I will be exalted in the earth. The LORD of HOSTS is with us; the GOD of Jacob is our refuge.

NKJV

SILENT NIGHT, HOLY NIGHT

On December 18, 1976, at 11:15 pm, I was talking to a Christian friend from Arlington, VA. Suddenly, I felt a pressure in my heart, and had to end our conversation, because I couldn't talk. When I hung up, the phone rang. It was my brother from Philadelphia, telling me that our father had just died. He died at 11:15 pm.

The next day, I sang a song that I had written a few weeks earlier. The words are, "Be still, my child, and know that I AM GOD. Enter into my rest, my child; enter into my joy; enter into my peace, my child; be still and know." The debut of that song had been scheduled for a week and was in the Church bulletin.

On the way to Philadelphia for the funeral, the LORD gave me I Thessalonians 4: 13-18 as words of comfort from the WORD OF GOD. "The LORD of HOSTS is with us; the GOD of Jacob is our refuge."

The LORD is reminding us to "Be still and know I AM GOD." Be quiet and listen, HE is speaking to you; sit still and worship HIM; clear your mind and your schedule so that the LORD has ownership of your time; rest in HIM and be at peace; HE is waiting for you in the silence of the Holy place within your heart.

The LORD goes before you and knows what you need before you know to ask. He is preparing the way for you to walk in the security of HIS love. Listen, HE is calling to you to come to HIM AND BE AT REST.

PSALM 47:5, 7-9

He chooseth our inheritance for us, The pride of Jacob whom He loveth. Selah God is gone up amidst shouting, the LORD amidst the sound of the horn. ⁷ For God is the King of all the earth; sing ye praises in a skilful song. God reigneth over the nations; God sitteth upon His holy throne.

JPS TANAKH 1917

A WORD FROM ME: I am amazed that this Psalm is in order for this week; the week which begins the High Holy Days for the Children of Israel. On Wednesday evening, the sound of the shofar will pierce the air. It will be a blast of triumph as the LORD GOD ascends on His Throne to shield His people. Kings and nobles will bow down before Him and will honor His Holy Name.

It is interesting that the United Nations has assembled in New York and today, heard the petition from Palestine to become a state. It is interesting that all the eyes of the world are on Israel right now. MAY THE GOD OF ABRAHAM, ISAAC AND JACOB BE GLORIFIED AND EXALTED FOREVER!

Do you believe that GOD is Almighty and able to shield you for harm? Do you believe that GOD always keeps His promises? Do you trust Him with your life? Revelation 12:11 says this, And they overcame him (satan) by the Blood of the Lamb, and by the word of their testimony; and they loved not their lives unto the death." We are victorious through the Blood of JESUS; we honor JESUS with our testimony of His great love; and we love Him more than our selves.

As the shofar blows the victory blast and all of GOD's people fall on their face before the King, JESUS Christ the LORD, let us shout, with them, the shout of triumph and watch the walls of the enemy come tumbling down.

PSALM 48:14

For GOD is our GOD forever and ever; He will be our guide even unto death."

KJV

A WORD FROM ME: I want you to ponder, with me, the last words of this verse: "He will be our guide even unto death." Do you/I believe that? Do you/I practice that in the daily life? What would it mean to live a life that had the LORD GOD as guide, counselor, advisor, and friend?

Most of us, if we are honest, would say that we consult GOD in times of real need. Well, aren't we all in "real need" right now? The times around us are a changin' and the questions that are asked, have found responses that don't seem to fit with our belief; people say strange things, fundamentals seem to be blurred. "I don't understand!" seems to ring from the bells in our heart. "Where is the answer? Who can give me guidance to live my life? What do I do now?" Do these questions sound familiar?

The answer lies in the first part of the verse: "For GOD is our GOD forever and ever." The LORD GOD has the answers and the way to follow, He has promised that He will never leave us or forsake us, but be with us always. His promises are "yes and amen" to all who believe on His Name. What is the problem, then?

The problem is that we have not because we ask not and when we ask, we ask amiss. Our Father who is in heaven, Holy is His Name, wants us to live well and be successful. He looks upon us with the eye and heart of love. We have been given access to the Throne of Grace through the Blood of JESUS, so we can come boldly into the presence of the King of Kings and LORD of LORDS. WHY DON'T WE COME? WHAT HOLDS US BACK?

Well, pride is one thing that keeps us from humbling our self before the LORD. "I can do that myself!" our little mind says. "I don't need help right now." WRONG. Every action has an equal and opposite reaction. A wrong move, now, can mean a series of errors later; the path taken now, precludes all other paths. What is the right path? JESUS said, "I am the way" walk in His path.

How do we change our behavior and what will it take to alter our process? There is only one answer:

PRAY, AND LISTEN TO WHAT THE LORD SAYS. FOLLOW HIS PATH AND LEARN FROM HIM.

PSALM 49:6, 7

They that trust in their wealth, and boast themselves in the multitude of their riches; none of them can by any means redeem his brother, nor give to GOD a ransom for him.

KJV

A WORD FROM ME: We are seeing on the news, daily, how our economy is in fragile shape; people are now demonstrating in the streets about the fact that there are some who are rich and others who are poor. Those with jobs are looked upon as the "rich" folk; while those without jobs are marching in the streets. The time is very volatile, it is not a time to trust in your riches or boast in wealth.

Where are true wealth and riches found? What wealth and riches CAN we trust? If earthly wealth and riches cannot redeem or pay the debt we owe, what can?

WE HAD A DEBT WE COULD NOT PAY; JESUS PAID

THE DEBT HE DID NOT OWE. True wealth and riches are found in Jesus Christ and we can trust Him with our life. The stain of sin was a mounting debt that kept us from fellowship with GOD; JESUS, the sin less one, redeemed us by His Blood and paid the debt that we had. Now we have fellowship with GOD through His Son, JES US. The ones who are rich are the ones who have given their life to JESUS. He supplies all the needs according to His riches in Glory, through Christ JESUS. These are the ones who give, and give and give, because of their gratitude to GOD.

He and He alone can redeem us from the awful debt of sin. JESUS IS THE ATONEMENT .

I am writing this on the Day of Atonement, Yom Kippur. On this day the Shofar will sound a long blast and a new year will begin for the Children of GOD. On this day, let us remember the long-suffering of GOD and His great Love that led Him to send His Son to redeem the lost world. He made the way open for us to come into His courts and worship Him. He is the King of Kings and Lord of Lords. May that blast of the Shofar be our triumphal shout of praise and thanksgiving for His great love. THANK BE TO GOD!

PSALM 50:10-15

For every beast of the forest is mine, and the cattle upon a thousand hills. I know all the fowls of the mountains; and the wild beasts of the field are mine. If I were hungry, I would not tell thee; for the world is mine, and all the fullness thereof Will I eat the flesh of bulls, or drink the blood of goats? Offer unto GOD thanksgiving and pay thy vows unto the Most High, and call upon me in the day of trouble; I will deliver thee, and thou shalt glorify me.

KJV

A WORD FROM ME: There is an old song, from the old Broadman Hymnal: "He owns the cattle on a thousand hills; the wealth in every mine. He owns the fields and the rocks and rills; the clouds and stars that shine. He owns the cattle on a thousand hills; and I know that He cares for *me*." There is not a sparrow that falls, that the LORD does not know about it. He even has all the hairs on our head numbered.

Everything that we see, GOD has created or given the way for it to be formed. Do you think that medicine was discovered by great thinkers? Who put the ideas in to the mind of man? Who knows how to use everything that is created for the benefit of man and animals; plants and the universe? Who is it that forms a baby in the womb of its mother, causes it to grow, and brings it into the world to grow into an adult? Who watches over us, with the LOVE that cannot die? Who defeated death, so that we will not die, but live forever? WHO IS IT? THE LORD GOD IS HIS NAME, JESUS CHRIST THE LORD.

"Offer unto GOD thanksgiving" for all that He has done for us. Thank Him for providing for our every need, even before we know to ask, and when we ask for help, He provides. Thank Him for His great sacrifice of Himself, in the "redemption of the world by our LORD JESUS Christ, for the means of grace and the hope of glory." THANK HIM, with all the gratitude of the heart of love, for He has done great things for us and Holy is His Name.

"And pay thy vows unto the Most High." Be faithful to Him for He is faithful to you. He will never leave you or forsake you EVER. Even if you are not faithful, He is faithful. The faithfulness of GOD is everlasting from generation to generation. He will not break His word to you. All His promises are "yes and amen." Now, pay YOUR VOWS TO HIM. You be faithful to Him in the same manner that He is faithful to you. Not for what you will get from Him, but that He will be glorified through your life. Our life is lived to glorify Him and serve Him with a grateful heart. In Matthew 25: 40 there are these word from JESUS: "Verily I say unto you, Inasmuch as ye have done it unto one of the least of these my brethren, ye have done it unto *me.*" Whatever we do to another, or to our self, we do it unto the LORD JESUS. THINK ABOUT THAT! He does not need food, but the hungry do; He does not need clothing, but the naked do; He does not need a house, but the homeless do; "whatsoever you do to the least of my brethren, ye have done it unto *me.*" JESUS says. When we look at another person, look closely, love deeply, and minister to their needs; THAT IS MINISTRY TO JESUS.

Your Thoughts:

PSALM 51:10, 15-17

Create in me a clean heart, O GOD, and renew a right spirit within me...O LORD, open thou my lips, and my mouth shall show forth Thy praise. For Thou desirest not sacrifice, else would I give it; Thou delightest not in burnt offerings. The sacrifices of GOD are a broken spirit; a broken and a contrite heart, O GOD, thou wilt not despise.

KJV

A WORD FROM ME: "Create in me a clean heart, O GOD, and renew a right spirit within *me."* Who is doing the work? Am I creating a clean heart by my own efforts and renewing my spirit by my own work? It is GOD who does the work within me to transform me into the likeness and image of GOD; that image in which I was created. (Genesis 1: 26, 27) We cannot form our self into the perfect image that GOD intended for our life. We do not have a clue as to what that image is; we may have a hint by our reading and understanding of the Scripture, the Holy Spirit gives us understanding and wisdom and knowledge, but we don't have a clue about the total image, only that it is the "image of GOD".

Having said that, there is One who does know what that image is and He, alone, can "create in me a clean heart" and "renew a right spirit". What does it take from us to open the way for GOD to reform us? Verses 15-17 give us the answer; "The sacrifices of GOD are a broken spirit; a broken and a contrite heart, O GOD, Thou wilt not despise." Let go of yourself and let GOD do the work. This sacrifice is the only one that matters to GOD. Let go of self, and let GOD do the work.

I had a word from the LORD early in my walk with Him; He said, "Yield unto me your concept of yourself, and I will fill you with My concept of *you*." This is the sacrifice that is pleasing to GOD. What it takes is a broken spirit; that is a spirit that will not rise up and challenge the work of the LORD. It also takes a contrite heart; the heart that is sorry for all of the sin that separates from GOD. It takes the yielding of all of our members to GOD, both outside and inside. That is our work, the work of submission to GOD.

You might ask, "Did JESUS have to do this?" If you look deeply into the Gospels and the Life and Teachings of JESUS, you will find that His whole life was total submission and yielding to His Father. Did He have an original thought, one of His own? Maybe, when He said, quoting Psalm 22:1, "My GOD, My GOD, why hast Thou forsaken Me?" This was a weak, human cry; His flesh cried out. But look at the Faith of JESUS when He said, "MY GOD" He was affirming His relationship with His Father, as His Son. Did JESUS yield to the Father and show us the way to live our life in righteousness? Yes, He showed us in every way, that it is through submission and yielding to GOD that we are cleansed and renewed.

LET GOD HAVE HIS PERFECT WORK IN YOU; YIELD TO HIM; LET GO OF SELF.

OUR LIFE, LIVED UNTO HIM, IS PERFECT PRAISE OF HIM.

PSALM 52:8, 9

But I am like a green olive tree in the House of GOD; I trust in the mercy of GOD forever and ever. I will praise Thee forever, because Thou hast done it; and I will wait on Thy Name, for it is good before Thy saints.

KJV

I HOPE AND TRUST IN THE COVENANT LOVE OF GOD.

A WORD FROM ME: One of the things that catch my eye about these verses is the phrase, "green olive tree in the House of GOD." What is that all about? Why is an olive tree in the House of GOD? To what is David referring?

The oil from the olive was used for the incense in the House of GOD and in the Holy of Holies for the daily lighting of the Lamp stand, by the Priest. Oil is used for anointing and cleansing. Oil is used in the Holy Offerings and is mixed with other significant ingredients to make a perfect offering unto the LORD. Holy oil is the symbol of the Holy Spirit. Since the Lamb of GOD is the Light in the City of GOD, JESUS is the perfect Holy One who is symbolized by the Lamp-stand and the oil is the Holy Spirit.

It is the mercy of GOD that we are given the way to be right with Him. Righteousness is manifest on so many different levels that we cannot be righteous in our own strength; He alone can make us righteous in deed and in truth. Our part is to TRUST IN THE MERCY OF GOD.

The next things that catch my eye are the words, "I will praise Thee forever, because Thou hast done it." GOD has done everything for us, all we have to do is live into what He has done. Our salvation was secured by the willing sacrifice of JESUS, who did not withhold anything, but gave freely for our salvation. "By His Blood, He reconciled us; by His wounds we are healed" everything is accomplished. HE HAS DONE IT; IT IS FINISHED. Our part is to praise Him, thank Him, trust Him; wait upon Him and know that He has done all that is necessary for our salvation, healing and restoration.

WAIT UPON THE LORD; WAIT, I SAY, ON THE LORD.

PSALM 53:1-4

The fool says in his heart, "there is no GOD." They are corrupt, and their ways are vile; there is no one who does good. GOD looks down from heaven on the sons of men to see if there are any who understand, any who seek GOD. Everyone has turned away, they have together become corrupt; there is no one who does good, not even one. Will the evildoers never learn — those who devour my people as men eat bread and who do not call on GOD?

A WORD FROM ME: The words, "will the evildoers never learn - those who devour my people as men eat bread and who do not call on GOD?" ring in my ears like a clanging bell. "When will they ever learn?" When will people stop hurting and destroying the great gifts from GOD? How long, LORD, how long before the evil will be driven out of the thinking and planning of people?

The answer comes in the coming of the Messiah, Jesus

Christ the LORD. The change in character, ways, thoughts and actions come when the LORD JESUS transforms a person into His likeness and image. "All we like sheep have gone astray and turned everyone to his own way, but the LORD laid on Him (JESUS) the iniquity of us all." In JESUS, those deadly, vile things are changed into life-giving good things; but, only if we turn to JESUS. "GOD looks down from heaven on the sons of men to see if there are any who understand, any who seek GOD."

When we are faced with questions, circumstances, disasters, and issues, to whom do we turn? Do we try to figure it out our self, using our own wits, and our own knowledge and understanding? There is a great saying that I hear often, "Make prayer your first priority, not your last resort." Go to JESUS for all understanding of situations and listen for His answer; then make up your mind to follow Him, where He leads. I would prefer to be 100% right than 50/50, wouldn't you?

Here is another saying that helps me to choose what I will invest my strength in doing; "Don't take on anything that you cannot saturate in prayer." Or, another way of saying it is, "Only take on those things that you saturate in prayer." When the LORD does the work, there is no burn-out or burn-up. When the LORD does the work, His will bring all things together for good for everyone.

CALL UPON THE NAME OF THE LORD; SEEK GOD; DO GOOD.

PSALM 54

Save me, O GOD, by Your Name; vindicate me by Your might. Hear my prayer, O GOD; listen to the words of my mouth. Strangers are attacking me; ruthless men seek my life; men without regard for GOD. Surely GOD is my help; the LORD is the One who sustains me. Let evil recoil on those who slander me; in Your faithfulness destroy them. I will sacrifice a freewill offering to You; I will praise Your Name, O LORD, for it is good; for He has delivered me from all my troubles, and my eyes have looked in triumph on my foes.

NIV

A WORD FROM ME: "Save me, O GOD, by your Name;" This is a cry that I am hearing every day from people who are in distress and their life is out of control. "Vindicate me by Your might," they cry day and night, unto the LORD." O LORD, help me and my family," "hear my prayer, O GOD; listen to the words of my mouth." "Are you listening to me, LORD?" "Strangers are attacking me; ruthless men seek my life." "Help me, O GOD" they cry day and night."

Notice the next words of this Psalm: "Men without regard for *GOD.*" This is a key to understanding the attacks on the Children of GOD. "People who have no regard for GOD," will do things that are ungodly to the People of GOD, who walk in the way of the LORD. The only way to defeat this attack is Spiritually. The battle is not ours the battle belongs to the LORD. If we can rest in the Almighty power of GOD and turn the battle over to Him, then we will see the victory. "Surely GOD is my help; the LORD is the One who sustains *me.*"

The shield of faith in the LORD is the part of the Armor of GOD that "recoils the 'fiery darts of the evil one'" (Ephesians 6: 16). Faith is the victory; we hold to the faith that the LORD will vindicate His people; in Him is the victory and to Him belongs the praise. We can hide in the "shelter of the Almighty" through faith and are shielded from the enemy by the Almighty Hand of GOD. He provides for and sustains His faithful people by His passionate love of the Father for His Family. Faith is the victory.

"I will sacrifice a free will offering to You." The "free will sacrifice" is a humble and contrite heart, yielding control to the LORD; letting go and letting GOD. We would like to have control of issues in our life; many think that they have to control things in order for them to work out well, but the truth is that the more we relinquish control to GOD, the better things will work out. We don't have the wits to defeat the evil one, but GOD does. When we let go and enter into praise of the living GOD; He acts for us. The hardest thing for people to do is to give Him ALL the control of situations. A very dear Evangelist once said, at a meeting that I attended, "We are like a parking lot, open to the LORD parking everywhere, EXCEPT where we have NO PARKING signs. Take down all the no parking signs in your parking lot and don't put them up again." She finished by saying: "Where are your NO PARKING signs? Pull them out, now!!!" I take that very seriously, when I erect a no parking sign, I immediately pull it up and throw it out; in the Name of JESUS.

PSALM 55:22

Cast thy burdens upon the LORD, and He shall sustain thee; He shall never suffer the righteous to be moved.

KJV

A WORD FROM ME: The last time that I wrote on this Psalm, I used this verse. This time, I want to go deeper into it and see what the LORD is saying to us, His people. There is a song that most of us have sung at one time or another:

"Cast thy burdens upon the LORD, and He shall sustain thee. He will never suffer the righteous to fall; He is at thy right hand. Thy mercy LORD is great, and far above the Heavens. Let none be made ashamed, who wait upon Thee."

Do you believe that the LORD will NEVER suffer the righteous to fall? Do you believe that He is at thy right hand? What you believe, is only a small fragment of the extent of the mercy of GOD. His mercy is far above the heavens and His love reaches to us. Do you believe that?

I say "yes" very quickly to the questions that I asked of you and of myself. Yes, I believe that the LORD will NEVER suffer the righteous to fall. However, when I fall, I say, under my breath, "Well, I guess NEVER is too strong a word; maybe "sometimes" would be better." I watch my belief erode, first by semantics and then by my speaking. Then I turn on myself, "Maybe I am not good enough to be called righteous. I am a worm and no man." Does this sound familiar? It is the 1,2,3, of the downhill slide.

THE LORD GOD WILL NEVER SUFFER THE RIGHTEOUS TO BE MOVED the Scripture says. The key is in the word, "righteous." This word means "to be rightly related". We are "rightly related" to GOD when we believe on the LORD JESUS Christ, because his Blood reconciled us to GOD. He broke down the wall of separation between us and Him by the willing sacrifice of JESUS. THERE IS NOTHING MORE THAT WE HAVE TO DO TO BE RIGHTEOUS. All we need is Him and to believe that He is the Christ, the redeemer of our soul. We are a part of the Family of GOD. Washed in His Blood and cleansed from the stain of sin. THANKS BE TO GOD!!!

The LORD GOD is at your right hand, watching over you, guiding you, healing you, restoring you, and believing in you. The question still remains, "Do you believe in Him?" He is the only one in whom you can put all of your trust. He is the only one who will never leave you or forsake you. He is the only one who knows the way to life everlasting. "Cast your burdens upon the LORD, and He shall sustain thee." Cast your life upon the LORD and you shall not be moved.

Your Thoughts:

PSALM 56:3, 4

When I am afraid, I will trust in You. In GOD, whose word I praise, In GOD I trust; I will not be afraid. What can mortal man do to me? JESUS said, "Let not your heart be troubled; you believe in GOD, believe also in me." Fear comes into us when we are not guarded in our heart. The heart that is filled with the knowledge of GOD and His Scripture will not be blind-sided by the work of the enemy or the misguided attacks of humans.

NIV

THE WORD, "WHEN", in this verse, reminds me that there will be times when I will be afraid. I know those times of fear, but I also know that a declaration of trust in the LORD dispels that fear. There are times when I have a dark dream in the middle of the night; I awake frightened. I have found that if I say the

Name of JESUS and a statement of trust, "JESUS, I trust in you." The darkness and the fear vanish and I fall asleep in peace.

The more of the Word of the LORD that I hide in my heart, the more I am able to combat fear; the more I praise the LORD, the more light is in me to dispel the darkness. The shield of faith is part of the armor of GOD and that shield protects the Children of GOD from the fiery darts of the evil one. Faith, trust and praise overcome fear, anxiety, grief and gloom.

What can mortal man do to me? The answer is, "nothing". Mortal man has no power to hurt or harm the Children of GOD, they can inflict pain and suffering, but cannot rob us of our soul when our soul is saved by the Blood of JESUS.

PSALM 57:7-11

My heart is fixed, O GOD, my heart is fixed; I will sing and give praise. Awake up, my glory; awake, psaltery and harp, I myself will awake early. I will praise Thee, O LORD, among the peoples; I will sing unto Thee among the nations. For Thy mercy is great unto the heavens and Thy Truth unto the clouds.

KJV

BE THOU EXALTED, O GOD, ABOVE THE HEAVENS; LET THY GLORY BE ABOVE ALL THE EARTH.

A WORD FROM ME: When we say, "my heart is fixed" "I will sing and give praise", "my glory", "I myself" "I will praise Thee" and "I will sing unto Thee" these are words of our choice. We, with David, have a choice as to how we live and what we think. Our choice is darkness or Light, sadness or joy, doubt or faith, control or trust, despair or joy. The Scripture, from the beginning, states a Word from the LORD, "Choose Life and you shall live." The LORD has set before us the choice of Life or death, blessing or cursing and He says, "Choose Life that both thou and thy seed may live." (Deuteronomy 30: 19)

"Thou and thy see" mark these words very carefully, your children depend on you being faithful to GOD. Our choices affect the life of those who come after us, to many generations. We are not walking this road as isolated creatures; there are generations that will spring forth from us that depend on our devotion to GOD and the path that He chooses. All through the Scripture, we find accounts of faithful people of GOD and how their offspring walked in the same path. Even the story of the prodigal son shows us that when a child runs away from the path of life, He will be drawn back by the devotion of the parent.

Mark these words: OUR CHOICE INFLUENCES OUR SEED TO MANY GENERATIONS. CHOOSE LIFE AND BOTH YOU AND YOUR SEED SHALL LIVE.

PSALM 58:1, 2

Do you indeed decree righteousness, you rulers? Do you judge the peoples with equity? No; you devise evil in your hearts, and your hands deal out violence in the land.

RSV

A WORD FROM ME: I really thought about skipping this Psalm and finding another more suitable for a New Year's Blessing. Instead, I asked THE LORD to enlighten me with words of wisdom from Him.

Everywhere you look there is corruption in high places, and we wonder what we can do about it. People suffer greatly at the hand of unrighteous leaders and they cry out for help. This is a fact in the world today. Rulers do not decree righteousness and people are not judged with equity. The blank stare of the uncaring person marks where their heart lives, in darkness.

As I read the rest of the Psalm, I noted that there is a

progression of perverseness in the heart of a man. It begins in the womb; estranged and perverted before birth. I see this as the thought life of an unrighteous person. They think and plan evil deeds in their mind be fore they begin to act perversely. This puts the matter on another plain; this is a spiritual matter, which is a prelude to the acts. Then, what we see and experience is born out of the sick, perverse spirit. The rest of the Psalm is about the LORD "breaking the teeth of the wicked" spirit within the heart of all people.

Righteousness means being "right related" to GOD. When we pray, "create in me a clean heart, O GOD; and renew a right spirit within *me*." We are praying to be cleansed from wickedness. Shouldn't this be our prayer for those poor, unrighteous souls who live in darkness, plotting evil things? Are they not slaves to the master of evil, satan himself?

JESUS came to set the captives free and to break every yoke. Let's join Him in prayer for the lost souls who live in darkness and who have been formed into groups of heart-slavery to evil. Let's join JESUS as HE SEEKS TO SAVE THAT WHICH IS LOST. Then all people will say, "Surely, there is a GOD who rules the earth" when the salvation of those souls is manifest.

PSALM 59:16, 17

BUT I will sing of Thy power; yea, I will sing aloud of Thy mercy in the morning; for Thou hast been my defense (stronghold) and refuge in the day of my trouble. Unto Thee, O my STRENGTH, will I sing; for GOD is my defense, and the GOD of my mercy.

KJV

A WORD FROM ME: "I will sing and make melody unto the LORD," these are not just words; they are the means to rise above all darkness into the glorious light of Christ. When we bring the sacrifice of praise into the House of the LORD, there is immediate release from darkness. "I will enter His gates with thanksgiving in my heart; I will enter His courts with praise."

The LORD is my defense and stronghold; He is a refuge from the pain and storms of life; He is the healer and the deliverer. All His mercy is the manifestation of His great love. In His mercy and love He brought His body as the perfect sacrifice for our sins and willingly offered Himself for our salvation and healing. Now we can bring our sacrifice of praise and thanksgiving boldly before the Throne of Grace and receive help in our time of need.

UNTO THEE, O MY STRENGTH, WILL I SING; FOR GOD IS MY DEFENSE, AND THE GOD OF MY MERCY.

PSALM 60:4

Thou hast given a banner to them that fear Thee, that it may be displayed because of the truth.

KJV

A WORD FROM ME: The word "banner" seemed to stand out for me as I read this Psalm. As I thought about this word, the song, "His banner over me is love" sang into my memory, so I stopped and sang it for a while.

I also read a commentary that was interesting, in that it prompted me to understand that trials of our faith are "opportunities" for strength and growth in the LORD. Yet again, I felt the need to go deeper into that word, "banner."

In an old Bible I found a cross reference to Isaiah 11: 10 it read:

> "And in that day there shall be a root of Jesse, who shall stand for an ensign of the people; to Him shall the nations seek, and His rest shall be glorious."

This is one of the prophecies of JESUS, the One who is of the root of Jesse, the House and lineage of David. Now, I feel that I have found an understanding of the "banner" that sets my soul singing. The "banner" is the Love of GOD and the "ensign" is JESUS, Himself. JESUS said, "If I be lifted up, I will draw all men unto Me." As we lift JESUS higher and higher, out of our love for Him and the souls of men, He draws people unto Himself and they are given the opportunity to confess Him as LORD.

An ensign is not only a "banner"; it is the insignia on the banner, the sign of the Cross of JESUS CHRIST. We carry the sign of the risen LORD JESUS and when we raise that banner high, we are lifted higher and higher by GOD, so that more and more souls will be saved. "LIFT HIGH THE CROSS, THE LOVE OF CHRIST PROCLAIM; UNTILL ALL THE WORLD ADORE HIS SACRED *NAME*."

YOUR THOUGHTS:

PSALM 61:2-4

From the end of the earth, will I cry unto Thee, when my heart is overwhelmed; lead me to the Rock that is higher than I, for Thou hast been a shelter for me, and a strong tower from the enemy. I will abide in the tabernacle forever; I will trust in the shelter of Thy wings.

KJV

A WORD FROM ME: These verses carry a very strong meaning for me. There have been times when I have felt overwhelmed and afraid. Then I cry unto the LORD and run, not walk, into the shelter of the mighty wings of GOD. There I can rest and be washed in the peace of the LORD. To abide there forever is my greatest desire, because the Love of GOD casts out fear, heals all wounds, cleanses from all sin and breaks the chains of bondage. It is my greatest desire, because I Love Him. There is a great rest for the Children of GOD, in the Tabernacle not made with human hands, whose maker and builder is GOD.

The LORD has said that He will give you the desire of your heart; my desire is to be with Him and worship Him for all Eternity. Do I have to die to abide in the Tabernacle forever? No, the Kingdom of GOD is within us, there is a place within the heart of each of us that can only be inhabited by JESUS. He invites us there to be with Him and to enjoy His Holy Presence. Yes, He waits for us to come and sit down, rest from our striving and be with Him in the glory of His Love. JESUS waits until we are ready to come, then He embraces us with such love that there is nothing to compare with it. The Love of GOD cannot be described in human language, but it is known by those who come and sit with JESUS and let the mighty wings shelter the trembling soul and give great peace.

As I was thinking about the "trembling soul," I remembered the little trembling Chihuahua puppy I saw. It trembled; its eyes filled with fear until its owner picked it up and carried it, huddled in his arms. This is what JESUS does for us; He picks us up, covers us with His arms, we can nestle down and feel the strong tower of safety. I watched that Chihuahua puppy fall asleep in the arms of its owner; I know that in the Arms of JESUS we can fall asleep in pure peace. When we arise from our sleep, He will be still there to guide us through the path of life He has chosen for us to walk. He said that He would never leave us or forsake us; He would be with us always, even to the ends of the ages. JESUS always keeps His promises.

PSALM 62:6-9

He alone is my rock and salvation, my stronghold; I won't be moved. My safety and honor rest on God. My strong rock and refuge are in God. Trust in him, people, at all times; pour out your heart before him; God is a refuge for us. (Selah) Ordinary folks are merely a breath and important people a sham; if you lay them on a balance-scale, they go up — both together are lighter than nothing.

CJB

FOR GOD ALONE MY SOUL IN SILENCE WAITS

A WORD FROM ME: I heard a saying that has stuck with me and builds me up when I think about it: "Faith is not believing GOD can, it is knowing that GOD will." The knowing that GOD will keep His promises; knowing that GOD is my hope, my Rock, my Salvation, my glory, my strength, my refuge; knowing that I can trust Him every moment; silences my fears, my questions, my doubts and my terrors.

We must grow in our faith to the place where we not only believe that GOD is able to do what He says that He will do, but know that when He says He will do a thing, He will do it. GOD is Almighty; He always speaks the truth; all power and authority is in His Hand; He hears the cry of the heart unto Him and He always responds.

There are two questions that JESUS asks the disciples after He rebuked the wind that threatened the little boat in which they were sailing. Let these questions sink deep into your spirit. JESUS said, "Why are you so fearful? How is it that ye have no faith?" (Mark 4: 40) What I hear JESUS saying is that faith is knowing that GOD can do what He says. He will calm the sea of trouble, change the circumstances and alter the outcome of things. What is our part then? Our part is to trust him every moment and pour out our hearts before Him, knowing that He is our refuge, our Rock, our strength, our Salvation and our hope.

Psalm 62 reminds us to wait upon the LORD. Wait for Him to fulfill His promises; wait, filled with trust, hope and the knowing kind of faith. When we look at the recorded history of the mighty works of GOD; when we remember how the LORD has worked in our own life and the life of our friends; when we read the accounts of the mighty works of GOD in other people; it is not logical to fear, for what can happen that the LORD cannot speak and cancel the work of evil? We belong to GOD and are a part of His family. Abba Father protects and keeps His own. You can trust Him with your life.

PSALM 63:1-8

O GOD, Thou art my GOD, early will I seek Thee; my soul thirsteth for Thee, my flesh longeth for Thee in a dry and thirsty land, where no water is, to see Thy power and Thy glory, as I have seen Thee in the sanctuary. Because Thy loving-kindness is better than life, my lips shall praise Thee. Thus will I bless Thee while I live; I will lift up my hands in Thy Name. My soul shall be satisfied as with marrow and fatness, and my mouth shall praise Thee with joyful lips, when I remember Thee upon my bed, and meditate on Thee in the night watches. Because Thou hast been my help, therefore, in the shadow of Thy wings will I rejoice. My soul followeth close behind Thee; Thy right hand upholdeth me.

KJV

A WORD FROM ME: I spent a long time pondering this Psalm, because it contains so much for us to see and to absorb in our heart. These verses are heart-felt adoration of GOD coming from the thankful heart of David. David had been forgiven much and knowing that He had been forgiven for His manifold sins, he loved deeply. This ado ration of GOD springs forth from him like a river of pure water. He is in the desert, physically, but his heart and mind are alive with the fresh spring of adoration.

We can learn a lot from David. When we are in a dry and thirsty land in our circumstances, yearning for deliverance from the waste land of darkness, our adoration of JESUS, beginning early and continuing throughout the day into the night, will lift the darkness and flood our life with the bright light of faith. Literally, our soul will be satisfied with marrow and fatness as our mouth is filled with praise from joyful lips. The LORD is right in our midst and He is helping us through the darkness, all we have to do is turn on the light by our praise.

I am caught by the words of the last verse: "My soul followeth close behind Thee; Thy right hand upholdeth *me*." Most of us, at one time or another, try to run ahead of GOD, as if He was moving too slow for us. We catch a vision of Him with us and we say in our heart, "Come on along with me, GOD, and be Thou my support and strength." Well, I think that, at times, we get things backward to our peril. When we run ahead of GOD, we are walking in darkness. We grope along feeling our way in the pitch black of unknown territory. Because GOD is with us, there may be a glimmer of light and we think that we see the path. BUT, if we follow close behind the LORD, we are walking in the pure light of His countenance and we are able to see the path clearly. Sometimes, the LORD walks the path slowly, sometimes he hurries along, but we must always follow close behind, not to the right or to the left and NEVER ahead. There is great safety in following the LORD; there is great uncertainty when we run ahead. The fear of the unknown is the greatest of all the fears. The LORD knows everything that was and is and is to come, if we follow close behind Him, we will have no fear, for He is leading the way.

THY LOVINGKINDNESS IS BETTER THAN LIFE, MY LIPS SHALL PRAISE THEE.

PSALM 64:1

Hear my voice, O GOD, in my prayer; preserve my life from fear of the enemy.

KJV

A WORD FROM ME: Who is the enemy of whom David speaks? Who is our enemy? Is it a person? Is it a place? Is it a thing? Does this enemy have power?

The enemy, I believe, is Satan, the enemy of our soul. Behind every diabolical act, there is the essence or spirit of the one who re belled against heaven and was cast out with his angels. When we begin to think this way, we begin to understand that "we wrestle not against flesh and blood, but against principalities and powers." We begin to understand that the battle is not ours to fight; the battle belongs to the LORD, who has all power to subdue the enemy. We can also under stand why the Archangel Michael did not rebuke Satan, but said, "The LORD rebuke you."

The enemy is very real and would like to convince us that he has power to kill, steal and destroy the things and people of GOD. I want you to look deeply into the verse that I just referenced from John 10:10: "The thief cometh not but to steal, and to kill and to destroy; I AM come that they might have life, and that they might have it more abundantly." Many people look at the first part of the verse and forget to remember the second part. Yes, the enemy comes to steal the Word of GOD, kill the body and destroy the soul of man, BUT JESUS came to bring life and that we would have that life more abundantly in Him. I believe that JESUS has already defeated the enemy, the Devil, by His willing sacrifice on the Cross. The Blood of JESUS reconciles us to GOD and we are saved when we believe on the LORD JESUS Christ. The enemy has no power against the Blood of JESUS; death does not defeat life in JESUS; JESUS defeated death and the author of death, Satan.

When we understand that the enemy is not a person, place or thing; when we understand that the enemy has no power, only the power we give him by our fear of him; when we understand that JESUS is the author of Life and All power and authority is His; THEN we will run to the shelter of JESUS and let Him deal with the enemy. The enemy is not big, mean and tough, that is an illusion that he projects; the enemy is small, weak and fragile, his only weapon is our own fear of him. We give Satan power by our belief in him as big, mean and tough. Faith in the LORD JESUS Christ, and in the power of His Blood, defeats Satan and binds his ability to torment. Yes, he uses willing servants to do his dirty work; BUT JESUS has given us a key to defeat him, "Love your enemies as yourself." When we use the key of LOVE, Satan crawls away like the coward that he is, he cannot love. There is another key that sends the enemy to flight, the Word of the LORD. JESUS used this key in the wilderness when He was confronted by Satan and the enemy fled.

My dear friends do not wrestle against flesh and blood to defeat them and vindicate yourself; the enemy is in the spirit, so say with the Archangel Michael, "The LORD rebuke you." Yes, we have been given authority to cast out demons, but let us not forget that it is far better to ask the LORD to defend us and we hide in the shelter of the Almighty. There are many Scripture stories about the LORD going ahead and defeating the enemy while the Children of GOD rested. The Apostle Paul is one of those whom the LORD delivered from prison while he was asleep.

People are not the problem; places are not the problem; things are not the problem; JESUS has defeated the problem and we are safe in the shelter of the Almighty, the Rock, the fortress, and our deliverer.

PSALM 65:1, 2

Praise waiteth for Thee, O GOD, in Zion; and unto Thee shall the vow be performed. O Thou who hearest prayer, unto Thee shall all flesh come.

KJV

To you, God, in Tziyon, silence is praise; and vows to you are to be fulfilled. You who listen to prayer, to you all living creatures come.

CJB

A WORD FROM ME: I was stopped in my tracks by the first words in both the KJV and the Complete Jewish Bible. "Praise waiteth for Thee," "Silence is Your praise, O GOD in Zion." An old KJV uses the word "silent" in place of "waiteth" and this caused me to wonder even more. Could it be that high praise is silence? What is there about this understanding of silence that our mind does not grasp? So, I went to the commentary from the ancient Rabbis to see what they saw in the Hebrew words of this Psalm. What I found was very sobering.

I found that the Rabbis consider this Psalm to contain a deeper theme: the ultimate Messianic redemption. Rashi explains "that any effort to recount all of GOD'S virtues is utterly futile, since His wondrous attributes are infinite. Indeed, every attempt to completely enumerate His praises only detracts from His glory, for it implies that His praises are finite and within human understanding." Rashi continues, "When man stands before his Creator in silent recognition of His own inadequacy, this constitutes the most eloquent testimony to GOD'S magnificence which defies human comprehension." I also see that the silence is wonder and awe at GOD'S Holy Love.

I used to sing a solo called, "The Heart Worships." The first words were: "Silence in Heaven, silence on earth, silence within. Thy touch, O LORD over all the earth, covers the din." Silence is high praise, because it recognizes the fact that words limit and silence expands. True silence acknowledges the truth that there are no words that are adequate to express the vast reality of the limitless love of GOD. There fore, to express true praise of the magnitude of GOD and His love for us, we can only sit in deep silence, with our heart overflowing in worship.

The Psalmist and the Rabbis await the coming of the Messiah in deep silence. The Christian knows JESUS as the Messiah, who is the redemption of our soul, and His Holy Spirit whom He sent to teach us all things and bring all things into remembrance whatsoever JESUS told us. Knowing JESUS, our Redeemer and Savior, causes me to look into the face of the Holy One and praise Him in silent awe. Could it be that silence is really "reverential awe"? Could it be that the "fear of the

LORD, which is the beginning of wisdom" is really Holy silence? "I wonder as I wander out under the sky, how JESUS the Savior did come for to die, for poor awnry people like you and like I? I wonder as I wander, out under the sky."

Today let your heart worship with the high praise of Holy silence.

Your Thoughts:

PSALM 66:1-4

Make a joyful noise unto GOD, all ye lands, sing forth the honor of His Name; make His praise glorious. Say unto GOD, "How awesome art Thou in Thy works! Through the greatness of Thy power shall Thine enemies submit themselves unto Thee." All the earth shall worship Thee, and shall sing unto Thee; they shall sing to Thy Name.

KJV

A WORD FROM ME: In the middle of winter time, when the air is cold in the morning and we struggle to arise from our beds to face a new day and its challenges; let us sing aloud these verses from Psalm 6 and let praises ring to GOD, who has brought us to the beginning of a new day. Thanks be to GOD for all that He has done for us; "How awesome art Thou in Thy works! Through the greatness of Thy power shall Thine enemies submit themselves unto Thee." All the earth shall worship Thee, the Father Everlasting and shall sing unto Thee and glorify Thy Name, O Most High.

If we would begin our day with this praise of GOD, all the day that will unfold before us, will be threaded by the praise of our lips. There is nothing that can befall us that GOD will not heal; praise of the LORD and honor given to His Name, ushers in the Presence of the LORD and His power to save. Doom and gloom ushers in the enemy; praise ushers in the LORD'S Presence. When we arise to the beginning of the gift of a new day, let us worship the LORD and give Him the day He has given us, so that all things will work together for good.

All the enemies of the LORD will submit to Him; He has the power over them. Who are the enemies of the LORD?

> *"We wrestle not against flesh and blood, but against principalities, against powers, against rulers of the darkness of this world, against spiritual wickedness in high places"* (Ephesians 6: 12).

When we embrace the praise of the Living GOD and glorify His Holy Name, all the principalities, powers, rulers of darkness and the spiritual wickedness MUST bow down and submit to the LORD. The Blood of JESUS defeated of all the dark forces of wickedness. JESUS defeated the enemy. In JESUS we are victorious.

MAKE A JOYFUL NOISE UNTO GOD, ALL YE LANDS. SING FORTH THE HONOR OF HIS NAME; MAKE HIS PRAISE GLORIOUS.

PSALM 67

*May God be gracious to us and bless us and make his
  face shine on us so that your ways may be known
  on earth, your salvation among all nations.*
*May the peoples praise you, God; may all the peoples
  praise you.*
*May the nations be glad and sing for joy, for you rule
  the peoples with equity and guide the nations of the
  earth.*
*May the peoples praise you, God; may all the peoples
  praise you. The land yields its harvest; God, our
  God, blesses us.*
*May God bless us still, so that all the ends of the earth
  will fear him.*

NIV

A WORD FROM ME: The Holy One has given us this Psalm and its hidden power to bring light to our life from the GOD of our salvation. We do not hear much about the Menorah, and yet, GOD saw fit to bring this seven branch candelabrum into the Temple. (Exodus 27: 31-40) The Scofield note says: "The Lamp stand is a type of Christ our Light shining in the fullness of the power of the Seven-fold Spirit. (Isaiah 11:2; Hebrews 1: 9; Rev. 1: 4) Later in the Revelation 21:22-24 we hear, "And I saw no temple in it; for the LORD GOD Almighty and the Lamb are the temple of it. And the city had no need of the sun, neither of the moon, to shine in it; for the glory of the GOD did light it, and the Lamb is the lamp of it. And the nations of them who are saved shall walk in the light of it, and the kings of the earth do bring their glory and honor into it"

I gave you the whole Psalm so that you could read and meditate on it. It was VERY important to GOD to give it to man, let us take it to heart as we pray it. This is a Psalm in which we intercede for the salvation of the earth and the nations of the earth. Today, our earth is in trouble because of the sinfulness of humankind. Wars are destroying the earth; evil men are destroying innocent people; we know that the destroyer is the devil, himself, who has come to steal, kill and destroy. Let us lift this Psalm as our golden menorah, and let the Light of JESUS Christ, the Lamb of GOD, light the seven-fold branches with the light of His Holy Spirit. The power of GOD will drive away the darkness of the devil and the "all the ends of the earth shall fear Him" "May GOD be merciful to us and bless us."

PSALM 68:1

Let GOD arise, let His enemies be scattered; let them also that hate Him flee before Him.

KJV

A WORD FROM ME: This verse from Psalm 68 is a quote from Numbers 10: 35b. The Torah contains much of the understanding that is reflected in the Psalms. This Psalm is part of the Messianic Prophecy which is fulfilled in JESUS Christ. This shadow of the coming of JESUS is confirmed by the words of the Torah and the Life and teachings of JESUS. All of the message of the Bible comes together in this Prophetic word, "Let GOD arise, let His enemies be scattered; let them also that hate Him flee before Him." JESUS, who is GOD, arose and defeated Satan and His works.

In this past few weeks, the words from an old hymn have been ringing in my heart, "Rise up, O men of GOD; have done with lesser things. Give heart and soul and mind and strength to serve the King of Kings ... Lift High the Cross of Christ, tread where His feet have trod. As brothers of the Son of Man, rise up o men of GOD." I am feeling that the call is to the Church of JESUS Christ, His Body, to rise up from slumber and prepare to join JESUS in the ongoing defeat of the enemy, Satan.

Notice that I said, "Prepare". We must be ready to speak the word of GOD to people who are "dying" to hear the truth. The Acts 2:42 gives a plan of preparation: Follow the Doctrine of the Apostles, fellowship in the Doctrine of the Apostles, continue in the breaking of the bread and in the prayers. We need to be more prepared than a football player, sitting on the bench, is prepared for the call of the coach to get into the game. We must study the Word of GOD, fellow ship with those of sound faith, Commune with JESUS in His Body and Blood, and pray without ceasing. The Church of the Living GOD is in slumber; JESUS is not slumbering, He is waiting for the Church to arise and "gird up the loins like a man". We are very much like Job, grieving over the losses in our world and our home rather that reach ing out in the only way that Satan cannot reach; unconditional love. Do we know how to do that? Or are we still asleep?

I listen to the rhetoric on the radio and TV and it makes me sick how things are ignored, explained away, denied, or argued; name calling has become an epidemic of hate words. Hate and lying are the hallmark of Satan, words of hate and lies come from the enemy him self. How do we overcome? "By the Blood of the Lamb, the word of our testimony and we love not our life even unto the death." (The Revelation 12: 11)

Satan cannot love or tell the truth, it is impossible for him to love anything or anybody. Unconditional love defeats any and all the maneuverings of the enemy and truth telling comes from loving so much that you cannot lie. We can only prepare to live the unconditional love life by preparing our heart in worship, study of the Word of GOD, fellowship, Communion and prayers. Let us arise and gird up our loins like a man and prepare to enter the arena of the spreading of the Gospel of JESUS Christ. PEOPLE ARE DYING TO HEAR THE GOOD NEWS.

PSALM 69:35, 36

For GOD will save Zion, and will build the cities of Judah, that they may dwell there, and have it in possession. The seed also of His servants shall inherit it, and they who love His Name shall dwell therein.

KJV

A WORD FROM ME: This is the last of the Messianic Trilogy in the Psalms of David. There are other Psalms which foretell the life of JESUS, the Messiah. The three Psalms; 67, 68, 69, are like a three panel picture. The next in order of the Messianic Psalms is Psalm 72. I want to quote the commentary from the Scofield Commentary, because it contains references that support the claims that this is a Messianic Psalm and picture of JESUS as the Messiah.

"The N.T. quotations from, and references to, this Psalm indicate in what way it foreshows Christ. It is the Psalm of His humiliation and rejection (vv. 4, 7-8; 10-12). Verses 14-20 may well describe the exercises of His Holy Soul in Gethsemane (Mt. 26: 36-45); whereas v. 21 is a direct reference to the cross (Mt. 27:34, 48; Jn.19:28-30)"

The verses which I quoted at the beginning are a promise to Israel and a reference to past deliverance of Israel. The LORD has promised to save Israel and Judah; its land and its people. They will possess the land and live in safety. Take notice of the reference to the Tribe of Judah, it is the tribe into which the Father placed his Son, the Lion of the Tribe of Judah. We must never forget that Israel and Judah are holy and precious, chosen by GOD for his very own. This is why we are to pray for the peace of Jerusalem, because prosperity follows those who love her. Christians are a part of the New Jerusalem, the Holy City where GOD dwells. We have been grafted into the Holy Vine, by our confession that JESUS is Lord of our life and GOD of our Salvation. The Blood of JESUS unites us to GOD and we are reconciled to Him by the Blood of the New Covenant. We must never forget the love that our Father has for His Children of Israel and Judah.

The last verse, v. 36, is a promise and a reference to the Pass over. First, it refers to the deliverance of the Children of Israel from Egypt, when the LORD instructed the Children of Israel to put the Blood of the Lamb on the door post and the lintel of the house and remain in the house while the LORD passed over. Death came to the houses where there was no Blood; where the Blood had been applied; all within the house lived and were saved. The promise for all the generations to come, is that the seed of the Servants of GOD shall inherit the land, and they who love His Name shall dwell therein (Revelation 21: 9-27). Notice verse 24 of Revelation 21: "and the nations of them who are saved shall walk in the light of it, and the kings of the earth do bring their glory and honor into it." Yes, those who Love His Name, shall dwell in the New Jerusalem.

JESUS reconciled us to GOD; He paid the price for our sin and redeemed us by His Precious Blood. His Blood is on the door post and lintel of the heart of those who love Him. What remains is our confession.

That we Love the LORD GOD with all our heart, soul, mind and might and say with the Holy Spirit, JESUS is LORD.

PSALM 70:4

Let all those who seek Thee rejoice and be glad in Thee; and let such as love Thy Salvation say continually, "Let GOD be magnified."

KJV

A word from me: LET THE NAME OF THE LORD BE MAGNIFIED. I have often been drawn to the word of the LORD recorded by Ezekiel. I often turn to Ezekiel 36: 25-28, 32a. This is the Word of the LORD to the Children of Israel and to us, His beloved ones:

"Therefore, say unto the house of Israel (and to us, also): Then will I sprinkle clean water upon you, and ye shall be clean; from all your filthiness, and from all your idols, will I cleanse you. A new heart also will I give you, and a new spirit will I put within you; and I will take away the stony heart out of your flesh, and I will give you a heart of flesh. And I will put my Spirit within you, and cause you to walk in my statutes, and ye shall keep mine ordinances, and do them, and ye shall dwell in the land that I gave your fathers; and ye shall be my people, and I will be your GOD Not for your sakes do I this, saith the LORD GOD, be it known unto *you.*" "But for mine Holy Name's Sake." (Verse 226)

All the wonderful things that the LORD has done for us can not be told in a few sentences. There are not words to thank Him for His Salvation from the judgment of GOD. It is through Him that we live and move and have our being. Yes, our very breath is from Him. Our only way to thank Him is to glorify him among the people, praise him in our heart and out of the abundance of our heart our mouth speaks. LET THE NAME OF THE LORD BE MAGNIFIED.

"Every good gift and every perfect gift is from above and cometh down from the Father of lights, in whom there is no variableness neither shadow of turning. Of His own will begot He us with the Word of Truth, that we should be a kind of first fruits of His creatures." (James 1:17, 18)

As we look toward the Holy Week and the road JESUS walked for our Salvation, let us not forget the price GOD had to pay for our Salvation. Let us not forget the pain JESUS had to bear; the Blood that was shed; the path to the Holy of Holies where the Blood was poured on the Mercy Seat for us. Let us not forget that JESUS did all this in obedience to the Father, who loved us so much that He would not let us die in gross sin. THIS IS THE FATHER'S LOVE THAT: "But GOD commandeth His love toward us in that, while we were yet sinners, Christ died for us. Much more then, being now justified by His Blood, we shall be saved from wrath through Him." (Romans 5: 8, 9)

Your Thoughts:

PSALM 71:16-19

My mouth shall show forth Thy righteousness and Thy salvation all the day; for I know not the number thereof. I will go in the strength of the LORD GOD; I will make mention of Thy righteousness, even of Thine only. O GOD, Thou hast taught me from my youth; and hitherto have I declared Thy wondrous works. Now also when I am old and gray headed, O GOD, forsake me not, until I have shown Thy strength unto this generation, and Thy power to everyone that is to come. Thy righteousness also, O GOD, is very high, who hast done great things. O GOD, who is like thee?

KJV

A WORD FROM ME: When I am filled with wonderful news, when I am in love with a person, when I have a terrific story to tell, I can't hold back telling everyone I see, the wonderful events in my life. I am sure that you are the same. I just bubble over and share the good news with everyone.

WELL, JESUS is the righteous one who has paid the price for all our failures and redeemed us from death. Shout it from the house tops; we are redeemed by the Blood of the Lamb of GOD. The LORD GOD loves us so much that He wants us to live with Him forever. His love provided the way for us to abide with Him and in Him. Shout it from the house tops that GOD so loved us that He gave his only Son for us who believe in Him. I have a terrific story to tell to everyone, JESUS IS LORD, GOD IS LOVE, HE HAS REDEEMED US, AND WE LIVE IN HIM.

I was taught the Scripture from my youth in a wonderful Sun day school, taught by men and women of great faith. Now that I am old and gray headed, I want, with all my heart for everyone to know that they are greatly loved by Creator GOD and his love is unconditional and merciful. I want all this generation to embrace JESUS and receive the free gift of Eternal life in Him. I don't want anyone to miss the message of Salvation that is through JESUS Christ the LORD. I say, with the Psalmist, "O GOD, who is like thee?"

For His Holy Name Sake we live, move and have our being, JESUS IS LORD!

PSALM 72:17-19

His Name shall endure forever; His name shall be continued as long as the sun and men shall be blessed in Him. All nations shall call Him blessed. Blessed be the LORD GOD, the GOD of Israel, who only doeth wondrous things. And blessed be His glorious Name forever; and let the whole earth be filled with His glory. Amen and Amen.

BLESSED BE THE NAME OF THE LORD; BLESSED BE HIS HOLY NAME FOREVER AND EVER.

KJV

A WORD FROM ME: Psalm 72 is one of the Messianic Psalms since it presents the vision of the Messianic Kingdom from the view of the Old Testament. Verse 1 refers the Coronation of the King's Son which gives Him the Kingdom; JESUS is the Son of

GOD having been given the Kingdom by the Father. Verses 2-7 and 12-14 give the character of the Kingdom, with the emphasis on the word "Righteousness" in verses 2,3 and 7. Verses 8-19 speak of the universality of the Kingdom, and His kingdom shall spread from shore to shore, from sea to sea and over the whole earth. THY KINGDOM COME, O LORD, ON EARTH AS IT IS IN HEAVEN.

The Name of JESUS "shall endure forever; His name shall be continued as long as the sun and men shall be blessed in Him." "All Nations shall call Him blessed." We might not see this manifested yet, it seems that this might be a long way off for the world to proclaim that JESUS Christ is LORD, but in a moment, in the twinkling of the eye, at the last trumpet, there will be a change. When JESUS appears so that every eye will see Him, every knee will bow and every tongue will confess that JESUS Christ is LORD, to the glory of GOD the Father.

When will JESUS return and when will all knees bow to Him? The Father knows and in the fullness of time, it will happen. What shall we do in the meantime? Watch and wait faithfully; do not turn from the way of the LORD; be faithful, fervent and be fruitful. We bear the Good News of the fact that JESUS came in the flesh and willingly died for us; He carried His own Blood into the Holiest place and poured it on the Mercy Seat in the heavenly place; JESUS reconciled us to GOD; He paid the price for our redemption. By Him, through Him and in Him we are Sanctified, Justified and Redeemed. We are His witnesses to the end of the earth, this is how we abide until He comes, by our testimony.

Sisters and brothers in Christ JESUS; be faithful, be fervent, and be fruitful; glorify GOD with your whole life and lift up the Holy Name of JESUS for He is LORD of all.

PSALM 73:1-3; 26-28

Truly GOD is good to Israel, even to such as are of a clean heart. But as for me, my feet were almost gone; my steps had almost slipped; for I was envious of the foolish, when I saw the prosperity of the wicked... My flesh and my heart fail, BUT GOD is the strength of my heart, and my portion forever. For, lo, they that are far from thee shall perish; Thou hast destroyed all those who play the harlot departing from Thee. But it is good for me to draw near to GOD; I have put my trust in the LORD GOD, that I may declare all Thy works.

KJV

A WORD FROM ME: Book III of the Books of Psalms begins with a confession of total weakness on the part of Asaph. Let me introduce you to Asaph: He was the leading Levite musician of his time and his name is often equated with that of David. He was more than a composer, he was also a prophet. 12 Psalms in a series in Book III, are attributed to him, he was a man who was strong in the LORD. But here, we find the confession of great weakness in this strong prophet/musician of Israel.

Asaph says that he is failing to keep his faith strong in the way of the LORD. He is tempted to join the way of the foolish, because they prosper. He is lured by the prosperity and fatness that the wicked experience, while he is suffering want and leanness. He says that he is envious of them.

In verse 21-24 he says, "Thus my soul was grieved, and I was pricked in my heart," as he laments his sin and his attraction to the way of the wicked. He confesses before the LORD that he is continually with the LORD and that the LORD has held him in His hand, giving him counsel and guiding him, leading him to glory after his long struggle on earth. As a side light, notice the reference to eternal life and the hereafter. He ends this Psalm with these words, "It is good for me to draw near to GOD; I have put my trust in the LORD GOD, that I may declare all thy works."

When we are troubled on every side by the apparent prosperity of the wicked and foolish; when it is a hard struggle for the followers of the LORD to succeed in this world; when It seems that all the forces of darkness are pressing in on the faithful; remember this: BUT GOD, is watching over His own; BUT GOD is our strength and song, He is our help in time of need; BUT GOD, has the last word and those who "play the harlot", departing from the faith, will be destroyed. What appears to be prosperity in the view of the world system, is poverty in the Eye of GOD.

When you are faced with weakness and struggle with the

spirit of envy over the prosperity of the wicked, remember "BUT GOD" will supply all your needs according to His riches in Glory in Christ JESUS. Stay strong, remain in JESUS, know that He is holding you in the palm of His Hand; He will never leave you nor forsake you; you are HIS CHILD.

GOD HAS THE LAST WORD!!!!!

PSALM 74:16

The day is Thine and the night also is Thine; Thou hast prepared the light and the sun.

KJV

A WORD FROM ME: In the midst of this cry for help for the people of GOD, there is a series of strong statements of faith; the one quoted is one of them. Everything created belongs to GOD, even the ground that we walk on; the sun, moon and stars belong to GOD, the earth and all that lives on it belong to GOD. Humankind is an invited guest in the created world and is the beloved creation, himself. How do we treat what GOD has created?

Think about it this way, GOD loved us first and then offered Himself to us so that we might be saved, healed, restored, forgiven, and made righteous so that we could live with Him forever. GOD did everything for us, all we have to do is to love Him with all our heart, soul, mind, and might, receive His goodness and pass it on to others. GOD put everything in place so that we would receive from Him the highest and the best. He gave His highest and best for us; He deserves our highest and best.

What is our highest and best? Our whole self, lived for Him. He made us in His image, a reflection of Himself. When we live our life in truth, we are His hands and feet touching the created world with His love. It is sad to say that many do not see themselves as made in the image of GOD. There are so many souls who have lost their identity as Children of the Living GOD. When we yield to JESUS and believe He has come in the flesh and died for us so that we could be born again, WE HAVE A NEW IDENTITY. Our name is written in the Lamb's Book of Life and we are GOD'S own person. Don't let anyone steal your identity; you are marked as Christ's own forever.

Troubles will come in this life. We will all experience circumstances that are trying and difficult, BUT GOD is over all, in all, and through all things He will prevail and so will His Children. We are sealed by the Holy Spirit; therefore, GOD is for us, WHO CAN BE AGAINST US.

Live into the life that GOD saw when He created you. Beloved, you are very precious to Him. Live in Him, Live with Him, and Live for Him.

PSALM 75:3

The earth and all the inhabitants thereof are dissolved;
I bear up the pillars of it.

KVJ

A WORD FROM ME: I realized, when I read this verse and looked at the whole Psalm, that I was seeing "End times prophecy." I sought the thoughts of commentators to support what I thought this Psalm was saying. The Wycliffe Commentary says, "This oracle from GOD gives the basis for the pronouncements which follows. It is at the appointed time when GOD will take His place on the judgment seat. His control of the universe assures that the judgment will be sure." The Matthew Henry's Concise Commentary looks at the history of when this Psalm appears. He notes that the Psalmist says that he will judge as one who has been given the awesome task of serving the LORD in truth, then Matthew Henry goes on to say: "Public trusts are to be managed with great integrity; those who judge must judge uprightly, according to the rules of justice, without respect of persons." Matthew Henry goes on to say, "This may well apply to Christ and His government. The world and all the inhabitants of it were dissolved by sin; man's apostasy threatened the destruction of the whole creation. JESUS bore the pillars of it; He saved the whole world from utter ruin by saving His people from their sins, and into His Hand the administration of the Kingdom... 'for He upholds all things by the word of His power,' Hebrews 1: 3." All agree that the "pillars" are the belief and life in GOD.

I am drawn to the words "appointed time, when GOD will take His place on the judgment seat". In the "appointed time" GOD sent His Son to be the atonement for the sin of the whole world. Through Him, the door of life was opened to all believers. Sin was and is washed away by the Blood of JESUS and through JESUS we have Eternal life. In the "appointed time" GOD will bring out of this earthly realm His Church, the body of all believers in JESUS. In a moment, in the twinkling of the eye, He will call His children home and He will great them. At that time, I believe, He will bring the believers to the Berna Seat to give the rewards for the works done on earth. He will give the crowns of righteousness for good works; this occurs after the rapture of the Church. I believe that those who are left on earth will experience great chaos and the time will be as the Psalmist said, a time of confusion and disruption; then the Second coming of JESUS. After this, JESUS will set up His Kingdom on earth and the righteous will be with Him. Sin will be judged and the wicked will be thrown out to live with the author of Chaos, the Devil himself.

Many people have questions and opinions about this Theology of the end times. I leave you with this thought;

wouldn't it be wonderful to live forever with the One who loves you so much that He gave His life for you? Wouldn't it be awesome to live forever with the GOD of all love; LIVE in LOVE eternally wrapped in unconditional love? Think about it, I did and found that wonderful life of love in JESUS.

PSALM 76:1

In Judah is GOD known; His name is great in Israel.

KJV

A WORD FROM ME: I was drawn to this first verse because JESUS was of the tribe of Judah and Jacob's name was changed to Israel. When I am curious about things, I go digging for answers. What I found was pieces of the history of the Jewish people and great lessons from that history.

This is a Psalm discusses King Chizkiyahu's response to Sennacherib's assault on the city of Jerusalem. King Chizkiyahu refused to praise GOD for His mighty works of deliverance of the people of Israel; instead, he claimed that when you study the Torah, you expect GOD to act on your behalf, so why praise Him. This failure to praise GOD cost Chizkiyahu favor with GOD.

In these notes, I want to look at a few things;

- The King neglected to praise GOD;
- The King acted with arrogance;
- GOD moved with might and His name was exalted among the nations.

When we neglect to praise GOD for His mighty work on be half of us, we will suffer great loss. That loss will be our relationship with GOD. The great willing sacrifice of JESUS for us, His shed Blood and His obedience to His Father should bring us to our knees in great praise of Him. It is unfortunate that many consider this awesome work of mercy and grace on the part of GOD, to be expected and therefore, not worthy of praise and thanks. Let us stop right now and give GOD the glory due His Holy Name, without Him there would be no salvation.

The King acted in arrogance by saying that the study of the Torah would bring him victory. Study and meditation on the Word of the LORD will give wisdom and understanding of the way of the GOD; however, it is GOD who works miracles and wonders out of His great Love for His people. The Scripture points us to GOD, but it is GOD who works and it is His love that motivates His actions. There are many who think that study will bring the blessings of GOD; the truth is that the blessings of GOD are from His heart of Love for His people.

When GOD moves in a mighty way, He moves out of His great love for each individual involved. The failure of one person does not stop the abundant love He has for all the rest. This is the prime motivation of GOD and JESUS manifested this in His whole life. John 3:16 says, "For GOD so loved the world that He gave His only begotten Son, that whosoever believeth in Him should not perish, but have everlasting life." For His Holy Name Sake let us praise His Holy Name with each breath, and love what He loves with all our might.

PSALM 76:7, 10, 11

Thou, even Thou, art to be feared. And who may stand in Thy sight when once Thou art angry?
Surely the wrath of man shall praise Thee; the remainder of wrath shalt Thou restrain. Vow, and pay unto the LORD your GOD; let all that be round about Him bring presents unto Him who ought to be feared.

KJV

WHO CAN STAND IN THY SIGHT WHEN ONCE THOU ART ANGRY?

A WORD FROM ME: I have been concerned for a long time about the casual attitude of people toward GOD, Blessed be He. I use the word "casual" to be kind, actually the word is "disrespectful" and even "blasphemous" The LORD GOD deserves our utmost and high est regard, respect, honor and praise. It is He who created all things; it is He who redeemed us from sin; it is He who saved us from His own wrath. Can we possibly "stand in His sight"? Isn't it more appropriate for us to be on our face before Him in humble adoration of His Great Name and His Great Goodness?

Look at verse 10:

> *Surely your wrath against mankind brings you praise,*
> *and the survivors of your wrath are restrained.*
>
> PSALM 76:10 NIV

I am impressed how all people will be drawn to give GOD the praise when confronted by adversity. I am equally impressed with the fact that "catastrophic setbacks" can be illuminated, given light, by "giving unto the LORD the honor due His Name. He alone is Holy; He alone deserves our Highest Praise.

In verse 11, the "fear of the LORD" is defined as "reverential trust, including the hatred of evil" [Scofield Commentary pg.609]. We are to pay our vows unto the LORD and bring unto Him the sacrifice of praise into His presence with reverential trust in Him and a profound hatred of evil ways. People who do evil things are the focus of GOD, for their redemption. We are to join Him in His heart's desire for all people to be saved and all to come to Him in adoration and thanksgiving. The LORD GOD will silence the wicked and pull out their teeth of wickedness; why, so that they will repent and turn to Him for heath and salvation. THINK ABOUT IT!!!!

PSALM 77:11-15

I will remember the works of the LORD; surely I will remember Thy wonders of old. I will meditate also of all Thy work, and talk of Thy doings. Thy way, O GOD is in the sanctuary; who is as great a GOD as our GOD? Thou art the GOD who doest wonders; Thou hast declared Thy strength among the peoples. Thou hast with Thine arm redeemed Thy people, the sons of Jacob and Joseph.

KJV

REMEMBER

A WORD FROM ME: What do you remember? What do you meditate on day and night? In your thought life, what do you think about? Do you think about your troubles? Do you think about the world situation? Do you wonder how we can fix the troubles that we see? Do you wonder about things and people; lies and truth; plans and programs? What occupies your thought time?

Asaph began his Psalm 77 with a list of woes. He is consumed with worry and trouble. Then he REMEMBERED the might work of the LORD and he began to meditate on those things. Asaph is letting us know that when there are circumstances in our life that are trying to consume us day and night, ripping our dreams apart and causing us emotional pain and torment, that we must turn our thinking and our meditation to the LORD and remember His ways. Asaph ends his Psalm this way: "Thou didst lead Thy people like a flock." (Psalm 77: 20a)

When we REMEMBER the mighty work of GOD, our belief that GOD is able to do more than we can ask or imagine is strengthened. It is in worship that the Holy Spirit will fill us with the faith that is from above and we can stand against the storms of life unafraid.

REMEMBER, with Asaph, "Thou hast with Thine arm redeemed Thy people". REMEMBER that JESUS is our Redeemer, sustainer, healer and provider. We are the people of GOD, the flock that He Shepherds. JESUS is our Good Shepherd, who provides for us all with Holy Love.

PSALM 78:1-4

Give ear, O my people, to my law; incline you ears to the words of my mouth. I will open my mouth in a parable; I will utter dark sayings of old, which we have heard and known, and our fathers have told us. We will not hide them from their children, showing to the generation to come the praises of the LORD, and His strength, and His wonderful works that He hath done.

KJV

A WORD FROM ME: When I look at my library, I am so very thankful for all the printed material I have lining my shelves. I have 24 Bibles; commentaries; Biblical Dictionaries and wonderful books on history, Spirituality and Theology. My shelves are full. If I have a question, I can go to many sources for the answer. Many people use the internet to look up data for their research. The data is limitless; anyone with a computer can access endless material.

In the time of Asaph, who wrote Psalm 78, the way that the history of GOD with His people was recounted in "oral tradition." When people would gather together to worship GOD, the mighty works of GOD were told; the commandments of GOD were read and the law was read to the people by the Priests. It was very important for the people to know the "dark sayings of old" which were taught them by their fathers, so that the generations to come would know the mighty acts of GOD and His great love for them. It was vital for the children to know GOD and to praise Him for His strength and wonderful works. The story of GOD was central in the life of the Children of Israel, they would talk about GOD in their homes, in the marketplaces and in the temple.

The ease of obtaining access to the story of GOD has only worked to diminish the importance of telling the mighty works of GOD. We have become lazy in our search for the depth of the wisdom of GOD. If the last sentence offends you, I am sorry, but I challenge you to think about your devotion to the Word of the LORD and your search for the depth of His wisdom. I am reflecting on my journey into the story of GOD; do I know His Heart, His mind, His way, His vision? Do I spend my time in prayer and dialogue with others about the mighty work of GOD? Do I have a passion for equipping the Children with the reality of GOD and His Covenant through His Son? Do I live the Story of GOD with a passion that draws others to Him?

I will be doing a deep reflection on the Holy Scripture, this Story of GOD and look deep into His mighty works, great love and tender mercy. This will be a very slow process, not read the Scripture in one year kind of study, but read, study and inwardly digest the Word of the LORD. This will bring me to great praise of GOD. I also want every word that I speak to me in agreement with the Word of the LORD. PEOPLE ARE DYING TO HEAR THE TRUTH THAT JESUS CHRIST IS LORD AND OUR REDEEMER.

"Go tell it on the mountains that JESUS Christ is LORD"

PSALM 79: 8, 9

Oh, remember not against us former iniquities; let thy tender mercies speedily meet us; for we are brought very low. Help us, 0 GOD of our salvation, for the glory of Thy Name; and deliver us, and purge away our sins, for Thy Name's sake.
FOR THY HOLY NAME SAKE.

KJV

A WORD FROM ME: You may have wondered why I sign off each word for the week from the Psalms with the words, "For Thy Holy Name's Sake". Some will see this as the motto of the Order of the Daughters of the King, but others will see this as the hallmark of these devotionals. Well, both are correct. The verses of Psalm 79 repeat this phrase: "for the glory of Thy Name" ; "for Thy Name's sake".

I believe that whatever I do, say, or think should be held under this standard and should not ever fall. If I cannot say, after I have spoken, "For Thy Holy Name's Sake." I have spoken amiss and need to repent. Oh yes, I do a lot of repenting, because words slip out without my catching them. I still hold up the standard.

There is another standard of speech that I hold dear; whatever I think, say, or do must agree with the Word of the LORD; if it does not, then it should not be thought, said or done. Again, I do a lot of repenting, because I do not always do what I know is in agreement with the Scripture. I still hold up the standard.

Asaph reminds us that the LORD GOD is our salvation; the GOD of mercy. It is the mercy of GOD that He gave His only Son for the redemption of the world. Mercy is one of the Attributes of GOD; that which He will always give, freely and abundantly. He also expects us to be vessels of mercy, not for our sake, but for His Holy Name's Sake. He wants us to be vessels of love, compassion, grace, deliverance, faith, mercy and healing/salvation; not for our sake, that we should receive the glory, BUT FOR HIS HOLY NAME'S SAKE.

PSALM 80:1, 3, 4, 7, 14, & 19

Give ear, O Shepherd of Israel, Thou who leadest Joseph like a flock; Thou that dwellest between the cherubim, shine forth...Turn us again, O GOD, and cause Thy face to shine, and we shall be saved. O LORD GOD of hosts, how long wilt Thou be angry against the prayer of Thy people?...Turn us again, O GOD of Hosts, and cause Thy face to shine, and we shall be saved...Return, we beseech Thee, O GOD of hosts; look down from heaven, and behold, and visit this vine...Turn us again, O LORD GOD of Hosts; cause Thy face to shine, and we shall be saved.

KJV

A WORD FROM ME: I went digging into the Hebrew text for insight into this Psalm and came away stunned by what I found. It seems that this Psalm is a progression through the exile times of Israel. Before I give away the meat of this devotional, I want to explain the meaning of the dedication to the Shoshanim. The Shoshanim, according to the Targum, means that the psalm was composed by the justices of the Sanhedrin, who carefully study the testimony of the Torah. This Psalm bears witness to three calamitous periods of Jewish History while they were in exile: The exile of the Ten Tribes; The Babylonian Exile; and the Roman Exile. This is why the justices of the Sanhedrin had to authenticate this Psalm. I discovered a hint of the coming of the Messiah, JESUS, and the coming of the Holy Spirit.

The first exile is of the Ten tribes who are referred to as the "flock" led by the Shepherd. In the Blessing of Jacob was given to Joseph (Genesis 49:24) he referred to GOD as the "Shepherd, the rock of Israel." The implication here is that Israel is under the protection of the Divine Shepherd.

Take notice that JESUS uses the Name, "Good Shepherd" when He says, "I Am the Good Shepherd; the good Shepherd gives His life for the sheep" (John 10: 11). Could it be that He was referring to the Blessing of Jacob and the prayer of the Ten Tribes in exile? He certainly was saying that the flock of GOD is under the protection of the Divine Shepherd and says that He is that One. Read John 10: 11-18 in the light of the fulfillment of the Blessing of Jacob and the term, "Shepherd, the rock of Israel."

Verse 4 of Psalm 80 begins the reference to the Exile in Babylon. Here, in the Hebrew, the Name HASHEM, GOD OF LEGIONS is used. Israel repents of idolatry and viewed themselves as one of GOD'S legions, one of the many groups and forces which function in order to do the will of GOD. The use of the Divine Name, HASHEM denotes a trinity.

Note the statement of JESUS about the fact that He could call to His Father and He would send twelve legions of angels in

Matthew 26:53, is JESUS saying that He is One with His Father, the HASHEM, GOD OF LEGIONS? Yes, He and the Father ARE One.

The reference to "face to shine, and we shall be saved," is interesting. When the children of Israel were oppressed, they were in spiritual darkness do they plead for the illumination of GOD's shining face to dispel the darkness. Here we find the cry for redemption through the Light of GOD, JESUS, to shine upon the darkness of humanity and redeem the world from bondage.

When the Children of Israel went into the Roman exile we find Israel referred to as the "vine" Again a fulfillment by JESUS who said the He was the vine and we are the branches in John 15: 1-14. In verse 14 of Psalm 80 we find the same plea to HASHEM, GOD OF LEGIONS to send His legions to preserve and rescue the legions of Israel.

The Psalm ends with the call upon HASHEM, GOD OF LEGIONS to "cause Thy face to shine, and we shall be saved." The commentary says this, "The final salvation will be permanent only if it is accompanied by intellectual enlightenment which results from Torah Study. The Prophet teaches (Jeremiah 31:32): 'This will be the covenant that I will make with the House of Israel after those days, says HASHEM, I WILL PUT My Torah into their innards and write it in their hearts and I will be their GOD and they will be My nation." This was fulfilled when JESUS sent the Holy Spirit to reveal all things that JESUS said and Who is the Spirit of the Divine One: Father, Son and Holy Spirit.

The final Salvation is permanent due to the willing sacrifice of the Good Shepherd, who gave His life for the flock; JESUS who is the Vine and we are the branches; JESUS Who is the Light that pierces the darkness of sin, death and the grave defeating the cause of killing, stealing and destroying through His Blood of the New Covenant. This Covenant is permanent, because GOD made it with JESUS, who is GOD and sealed it with the Blood of His Son, JESUS. It is an Eternal Covenant; those who enter into it will be saved for all eternity. BELIEVE ON THE LORD JESUS CHRIST AND YOU SHALL BE SAVED AND YOUR HOUSE.

YOUR THOUGHTS:

PSALM 81:1-4

Sing aloud unto GOD, our strength; make a joyful noise unto the GOD of Jacob. Take a psalm, and bring hither the timbrel, the harp with the psaltery. Blow the trumpet in the new moon, in the time appointed, on our solemn feast day. For this was a statute for Israel, and a law of the GOD of Jacob.

KJV

A WORD FROM ME: I am learning so much from reading these Psalms from the Hebrew. I get excited as I read what was in the thoughts of the Psalmist, as he wrote down the words, and the tradition which has evolved from the understanding of the times. Asaph wrote from his heart; David wrote from the heart of GOD and the passion of his own heart; Moses wrote Psalms greatly inspired by GOD and the deep love he had for his LORD; the sons of Korah wrote from the passion of their own conversion. WOW, what great lessons we can learn from these men of GOD!

Psalm 81 is designated to accompany the Temple sacrifices on Rosh Hashanah. It is also the song of the day, the fifth day of the week. "On Rosh Hashanah, GOD showed that He was our might because He no longer allowed the Egyptians to enslave us. This event was a cause for joyous song" (Radak) "The Talmud designates this psalm as the Song of the Day...On the fifth day of creation, GOD made the birds and the fish, which bring joy to the world. When people observe the vast variety of colorful birds and fish, they are awed by the tremendous scope of GOD's creative ability, and they are stirred to praise Him with song. (Rashi, Rosh Hashanah, 31.a)"

I found that the instruments used in this Psalm were very interesting. The Gittis was a stringed instrument made in the town of Gat. In the Hebrew, the instruments in verse 2 are the timbrel, the sweet Kinnor with Neivel. The Kinnor is a harp, with the understanding that "the music arouses the inner spirit of the intellect and enhance its faculties (Radak)." The Neivel Assor produces ten different tones, Iban Ezra says it was a wind instrument of ten holes... the Midrash says, "It is called Neivel because its exquisite music makes all other instruments seem to be worn out, disgraced, withered." It is noteworthy that the finest instruments available were used in the Temple worship. The Commentators used great care in giving honor to the instruments of worship. I reflected on this and have come to the understanding that only the best should be used to glorify GOD. We must give our best to the Master, not just something we picked up, or we "bang on". This understanding gave birth to the great organs of the Cathedrals and the beautiful music of the Orchestras with the individual instruments of the finest quality. The LORD GOD should be honored with our best.

The first day of the month is called new, because the moon which waned and disappeared at the end of the previous month then reappears and begins a new cycle. Rosh Hashanah, which occurs on the first day of Tishrei, also coincides with the renewal of the moon. It is the only one of all the Jewish festivals which occurs at this time of the month. The shofar is blown on Rosh Hashanah to commemorate the cessation of the Israelites' slavery on that day. Similarly, the shofar blast is blown on Yom Kippur of the Jubilee year as a sum mons to liberate slaves (Leviticus 25: 9). This is established by GOD as a "statute for Israel, and a law of the GOD of Jacob" (Psalm 81: 4).

I have been a part of High Holy Days in the Temple and have heard the blast of the Shofar. In my thoughts, I hear the sound of that mighty Shofar blown as JESUS comes again for His Bride, the Church. There is no sound on earth like that sound and in heaven that trumpet or shofar sound would break any silence with a shout of great Holy Joy.

MAKE A JOYFUL NOISE UNTO THE LORD ALL YE LANDS; SERVE THE LORD WITH GLADNESS AND COME BEFORE HIS PRESENCE WITH A SONG.

PSALM 82:8, 3, 4

Arise, O GOD, judge the earth; for Thou shalt inherit all nations.
Defend the poor and fatherless; do justice to the afflicted and needy. Deliver the poor and needy; rid them out of the hand of the wicked.

KJV

A WORD FROM ME: These verses touch me as I read this Psalm. Verse 6 calls us all to "arise" and take hold of the LORD GOD as His Children. We are called to defend the poor and fatherless; to do justice to the afflicted and needy. We are called to deliver the poor and needy and rid them out of the hand of the wicked. READ ISAIAH 58, we are called to be the repairers of the breach, the restorer of paths to dwell in (Isaiah 58: 12).

Throughout the Scripture, the LORD calls us to defend the fatherless and the widow; the poor and the needy. We are the branch of the Vine of GOD, reaching out to the world with the

Blood of JESUS in our veins. JESUS reached out to those who were suffering, yes, to us who were suffering; He laid down His life for His friends and brought SALVATION through His Blood. NOW, we have work to do, the poor are crying out to GOD for help. Arise, Children of GOD and be the arms and legs and HEART of GOD; reaching, ever reaching out with His Love to all.

RISE UP, O PEOPLE OF GOD; HAVE DONE WITH LESSER THINGS. GIVE HEART AND SOUL AND MIND AND STRENGTH; TO SERVE THE KING OF KINGS.

PSALM 83:1-6

O God, keep not Thou silence; Hold not Thy peace, and be not still, O God. For, lo, Thine enemies are in an uproar; And they that hate Thee have lifted up the head. They hold crafty converse against Thy people, And take counsel against Thy treasured ones. They have said: 'Come, and let us cut them off from being a nation; That the name of Israel may be no more in remembrance.' For they have consulted together with one consent; Against Thee do they make a covenant;

JPS TANAKH 1917

A WORD FROM ME: I am tempted to become political in my remarks, but I will not do that. Instead, I want us to look at our own selves and see where our faith and work are focused.

The Psalmist, Asaph, is very clear that the things done on earth are done unto the LORD, whether good or evil. Those who hate us hate the LORD first; those who love unconditionally have the gracious Love of GOD in them. Yes, when we say, "We hate", we are not speaking in accordance with the way of the LORD. There is one thing that the LORD hates, evil, that spirit of evil that He cast out of heaven. The LORD loves unconditionally and hates evil, and so must we.

That being said, I am reminded that evil does exist in the world, how are we to respond to this evil? We are to recognize, with this Psalmist, that the evil done is against the LORD. The LORD will defend His Throne, He did it before the world was created, He did it throughout history and He will do it until the end of time. Though wickedness makes a covenant or a confederacy against the LORD, they will not prevail. GOD IS MIGHTIER THAN ANY CONFEDERACY, think of the tower of Babel and its end.

How do we pray in the times when the LORD is being de famed and blasphemed? "O GOD, do not hold Yourself silent; be not deaf and be not still, O GOD." Defend the cause of right and bring down the wrong so that those who practice wrong will be converted and THY NAME GLORIFIED.

The last verse of Psalm 83 says this: "Then they will know that You, whose Name is HASHEM, are alone, Most High over all the earth." This is the whole purpose of our being here, at this time on the earth. We are to make known the Name of the LORD and to live according to His way and His truth. We are to set the standard of the LORD before the people and call all people to "choose this day who you will serve"

The LORD has set before us life and death and He shouts, out of His great love, "Choose life and you will live." He asks us to be a " life line" to all others, holding out the hand of salvation to a world trapped by the evil one. JESUS paid the debt that He did not owe so that we would be free to come to Him. He bridged the gap between GOD and man so that we can come boldly to the Throne of grace and receive mercy. We must be vessels of that mercy and grace to others. Evil is defeated by unconditional love, mercy and grace. Let us arise and go forth to conquer evil by the Love of GOD shed abroad in our hearts through Christ JESUS. Throw out the life line to those who are sinking in the mire of wrong choices. Do not hate them, love them to JESUS.

PSALM 84:10 - 12

For a day in Thy courts is better than a thousand. I had rather be a doorkeeper in the house of my GOD, than to dwell in the tents of wickedness. For the LORD GOD is a sun and shield; the LORD will give grace and glory. No good thing will He withhold for them that walk uprightly. O LORD of hosts, blessed is the man who trusteth in Thee.

A WORD FROM ME: The first 2 verses of this Psalm are written in my mind and heart, because of the very famous Anthem, "How Lovely is Thy dwelling place, O LORD of Hosts. My flesh longeth, yea fainteth for the courts of the LORD. My soul and body crieth out, yea for the living GOD. How lovely, how lovely is Thy dwelling place, O LORD of Hosts" Those among us, who are Choir singers or were in a mixed voice ensemble, will instantly recognize this Anthem. There are many people who have asked for this to be sung at their funeral, because it means so much to them that they want to share it with others.

I have chosen the last verses of this Psalm as a testimony of dedication to the LORD. In my life, I have found that the days spent in the Courts of the LORD are my very best times. I love being in the House of GOD, even if I am there with only the LORD and His Holy Spirit. I love being alone with the LORD in deep prayer, soaking in His presence and resting in His love. I love being nestled in His arms when I sleep. I would choose to be in the House of GOD welcoming in those who are looking for JESUS; looking for help in their time of need or just hungry for the Word of the LORD. The warmth of the presence of JESUS is like the sun shining in my heart and like a shield from all harm; He gives grace and new life in every moment spent in His presence. The negativity of the outside world is so sharp and stingy; bitter and angry; that I would rather stay within the Courts of the LORD than gather in the tents of wickedness.

Notice the promise of GOD in the last verse of this Psalm, "No good thing will He withhold from them that walk upright!" With the eye of that wonderful gift of faith that is given by the Holy Spirit, I believe that what the LORD has promised, He will perform forever. No good thing will He withhold from those who spend their time in right relationship with Him; feasting upon His riches and dwelling in His Courts.

Trust in the Lord, my friends, and lean not unto your own understanding. In all your ways acknowledge him, and he will direct your path. Proverbs 3:5, 6

PSALM 85:10, 11

Mercy and truth are met together; righteousness and peace have kissed each other. Truth shall spring out of the earth, and righteousness shall look down from heaven.

KJV

A WORD FROM ME: I am struck by the Messianic nature of these passages. They speak to me of the life of JESUS, the Messiah, and His path of redemption for us. "Mercy" was obtained for us by JESUS carrying His own Blood and pouring it on the Mercy Seat in the Holy of Holies; "truth" is JESUS, Himself. He is the way, the truth, and the life; "Mercy and Truth Kissed when JESUS completed the work of Grace, through the willing sacrifice of Himself, out of Love for His Father and love for us. There is a bond between mercy and truth that cannot be broken; it is an everlasting Covenant of Blood and Love between GOD and Man through the man Christ JESUS, who is GOD incarnate.

"Truth" who is JESUS, the Son of GOD, sprung forth from the earth and "Righteousness," which is the Father GOD, looked down from heaven. When the work on earth was completed with the shout from the Cross, "It is Finished!" then Truth and Righteousness united into one person, JESUS. The separation was sealed by the Blood of JESUS poured out upon the Mercy Seat and then Mercy and Truth kissed each other. Now, through JESUS, we have access to the Throne of Grace, where we obtain mercy.

Was there ever a separation between JESUS and His Father? Yes, when JESUS took on Himself all the sin of the world and nailed it to the Cross. He bore our sin upon the Cross so that we would not suffer the penalty; "by His stripes He reconciled us; by His wounds we were healed." "IT IS FINISHED!" THE WORK OF REDEMPTION HAS BEEN ACCOMPLISHED THROUGH JESUS.

THIS IS AN EVERLASTING, UNBREAKABLE COVENANT AND WE ARE RECIPIENTS OF IT THROUGH JESUS CHRIST THE LORD.

Your Thoughts:

PSALM 86:1, 2, 11-13

Hear, o Lord and answer me, for I am poor and needy
Guard my life for I am devoted to you.
You are my God; save your servant who
Trust in you...Teach me your way Lord and I will walk
   truth;
Give me an undivided heart that I may fear your
   name, I will praise you
O Lord my God with all my heart, I will glory in your
   name forever.

NIV

A WORD FROM ME: This Psalm is a prayer when he is in deep distress. He declares his faith in God and his trust in the Lord whom he loved, in the midst of trouble.

Through the Psalm, he uses words of comfort and strength. Words such as guard my life; have mercy bring joy you are forgiving and good; teach me your way give me an undivided heart. I will praise you. And there are many more in this Psalm.

When we walk through troubled times and it seems that the world is against us and there is no hope David reminds us to use the word of encouragement. These are found in scripture and in the words of our own heart words that speak of the glory of God.

Words that build up the foundations of our faith in the only one who has the power to save. There is no trouble too great that the Lord God cannot bring salvation.

Trust Him.

PSALM 87:6, 7

*The LORD shall count, when He writeth up the people,
THAT THIS MAN WAS BORN THERE. Selah
The singers as well as the players on instruments shall
be there; all my springs are in Thee.*

KJKV

A WORD FROM ME: This is one of these passages that make my heart sing with the glad song of the born-again soul. When the LORD counts His people, the children who belong to the family of GOD, He will say, "You were born into my family." It does not matter from what realm you came; it does not who your family on earth is; it does not matter the former landscape of your life; what matters to GOD is that you were BORN AGAIN INTO THE FAMILY OF GOD.

Some may say, "What can I do to be born again?" The truth is that the preparation has already been made by the finished work of JESUS. His Blood has reconciled us to GOD. All you need to do is, "Believe on the LORD JESUS Christ and you shall be saved." Nicodemus asked that same question to JESUS (John 3:1-21) and JESUS told Him that what is of the flesh remains of the flesh, but what is of the Spirit is of the Spirit. You must believe on the LORD JESUS Christ who has made it possible for you to be born anew. Jesus said, "Verily, verily, I say unto you, except a man be born again, he cannot see the kingdom of GOD." (John 3:3) JESUS goes on to say, "Verily, verily, I say unto thee, except a man be born of water and of the Spirit, he cannot enter into the kingdom of GOD." (John 3:5) If JESUS thought and taught that it was of utmost importance to be born again, then we should take this VERY SERIOUSLY.

God so loved the world that He gave His only begotten Son, that who soever believeth in Him should not perish, but have everlasting life. For GOD sent not His Son into the world to condemn the world, but that the world through Him might be saved. He that believeth on Him is not condemned; but he that believeth not is condemned already, be cause he hath not believed in the Name of the only begotten Son of GOD. (John 3:16-18)

LOVE THE LORD JESUS CHRIST WITH ALL YOUR HEART, SOUL, MIND AND MIGHT; BELIEVE ON HIS HOLY NAME AND BE SAVED, YOU AND YOUR HOUSEHOLD. Sing and dance for joy; play on your instruments of praise for the LORD has redeemed His people and counted them as part of the family of GOD. Draw from the fresh water springing up within you from the Holy Spirit and sing aloud the praises of the LORD.

PSALM 88:1, 2

*O Lord, God of my salvation, I have cried out day and
night before You.
Let my prayer come before You; Incline Your ear to
my cry.*

NKJV

A WORD FROM ME: I have found, in my study and in worship in the Temple, that the Children of Israel have a very profound understanding of GOD as their savior. Sforno writes, "O GOD, You are responsible for every salvation I have experienced throughout my lifetime". The Midrash Shocher Tov includes a dialogue between Israel and GOD: "Israel said to the Holy One, Blessed is He, 'Our hopes and aspirations are concentrated on You alone!' GOD responded, 'In that case, I am compelled to save you!"

Salvation, to the Jewish people, is seen as a matter of relationship with GOD. They are His people and GOD is the GOD who saves them and leads them. They are the flock of GOD and He is their Shepherd. It is GOD who redeems them and delivers them from all the oppression of the enemy. GOD is the one who prospers them, giving them water and food in the desert. When they cry unto the LORD, He responds by giving Himself to them, because of the relationship He has with them, a relationship of profound love. He is their Father and they are His Children.

We know that JESUS is GOD incarnate. He brings all those who believe on His Name, into the relationship with GOD the Father that brings Salvation. The relationship between the individual and GOD means that the LORD will save them, lead them, redeem them, de liver them and prosper them. He responds to their cry because of the relationship He has with them; a relationship made possible through the shed Blood of JESUS and His willingness to be the sacrificial Lamb for our salvation. JESUS bridged the gap between GOD and man. The Covenant was sealed with His Blood. Since JESUS is GOD, that Covenant was made between GOD and GOD, therefore, it will never be broken; it is Eternal. The Born again relationship is Eternal.

When the Jewish people were in exile, they labored for their masters during the day. Day labor was hard and harsh for them. In the night, when they returned home, they spent their time in family communication; study of Torah, the Word of the LORD; prayer time and the LORD was present. When the Psalmist says: "by night I am before You," He is speaking about this time of sanctification unto the LORD. You might say that the LORD was present all through the day and the night, and this is correct. What the Psalmist is saying is that the attention was turned to GOD during the night. I find this thought very interesting. In Proverbs 3:6 it says, "In all thy ways acknowledge

Him and He will direct thy path." We are never out of sight of the LORD, He is always present; we only have to acknowledge Him.

When we acknowledge Him, He directs our path because of the relationship we have with Him (He is our Father, we are His Children). So, day and night we are before Him. When we confess Him as LORD of our life and GOD of our salvation, He receives us, because He loves us. BELIEVE ON THE LORD JESUS CHRIST AND YOU SHALL BE SAVED; AND YOUR HOUSEHOLD. BELIEVE IN JESUS AND BE BORN INTO THE HOUSEHOLD OF GOD.

PSALM 89:1-43 35-37

> *I will sing of the Lords love forever; with my mouth I will make you faithfulness known through all generations. I will declare that your love stands firm forever the you establish your faithfulness in you said, "I have made a covenant my chosen one, I have sworn to David my servant I will establish your line forever and make your throne firm through all generations."*
>
> NIV

"Once for all, I have sworn by my holiness and I will not lie to David that this line will continue forever and his throne endure before me like the sun; It will be established forever like the moon the faithful witness in the sky."

A word from me Psalm 89 is a declaration of David's covenant between God and David. It is an everlasting covenant established in the "heavens itself". This covenant paths the way and announces that the descendants of David would sit on the throne of God. Jesus is of the house and lineage of David.

Not only was Jesus of the house and lineage of David but of Mary and Joseph were of the same lineage. God prepared the way for the Son of God to be born in a Holy Covenant family.

It is also true for us. We have been chosen by God before our birth, to be a past of the family of God. It is the will that shall be saved from the consequences of sin, which is death. It is our choice He stands at the door knocking when we open the door He will come in and become our Savior and Lord changing us into His likeness and image.

Jesus, the perfect lamb of God willingly lay down His life, so that death would be defeated, and life would be ours. His blood reconciles us to God. Believe in Jesus and you will be saved.

The Psalm ends with these words in verse 52: "Praise be to the Lord forever! Amen and Amen."

PSALM 90:1, 2:17

Lord, you have been our dwelling place throughout all generations. Before the mountains were born or you brought forth the earth and the world, from everlasting to everlasting you are God.
"May the favor of the Lord our God rest on us; establish the work of our hands for us - yes, establish the work of our hands."

NIV

A WORD FROM ME: In the prayer of Moses the great man of God called by God to lead the people of Israel we find a declaration of the eternal God and His nature. You hear Moses recount the power of Almighty God and the weakness of humankind; He calls upon God to teach us to number our days aright that we may gain a heart of wisdom. (vs12)

We have a short time on here on earth; a short time to make

the glory of the Lord revealed to the world. Moses reminds us to make every moment count.

"Lord establish the work of our hands" Psalm 90:17

Your Thoughts:

PSALM 91:1

He that dwelleth in the secret place of the Most High shall abide under the shadow of the Almighty.

KJV

A WORD FROM ME: This is the second Psalm attributed to Moses and is dedicated to the Tribe of Levi.

What does it mean to "dwell" and "abide"? It means to live in or reside. Those who live in and reside in GOD are protected and sustained by GOD; He is Father of the household. As Father of the house, He delivers from danger, protects, saves, provides and guards both day and night. GOD, our Father never slumbers or sleeps and is always watching out for His children. It is our devotion to Him and our faithfulness to Him that keeps us in the shelter of the Most High.

How do we remain in the covering of GOD? We remain in the covering of GOD, the shelter of the Almighty, the fortress and under the wings of GOD, by our focus. When we focus on the LORD, love Him with all our heart, read and study His Word and pray, talking to Him as one who is ever present, then we will be sheltered by Him. Proverbs 3:6 says, "In all thy ways acknowledge Him, and He will direct thy path." Acknowledge means to recognize or to greet; literally to see. Do we see GOD with us? Do we greet GOD as The One who remains with us forever? Do we recognize Him as walking with us during our day and as we sleep at night, He is watching? If we "acknowledge Him, He will direct our path". He is the faithful Father who never leaves His child.

I will end with the last three verses of this Psalm, the words of which are the prophecy of the coming of the Savior, JESUS Christ: "Because he hath set his love upon Me, therefore will I deliver him; I will set him on high, because he hath known My Name. He shall call upon Me, and I will answer him. I will be with him in troubles; I will deliver him, and honor him. With long life will I satisfy him, and show him My salvation."

PSALM 92:1-4

It is a good thing to give thanks unto the LORD, and to sing praises unto Thy Name, O Most High; to show forth Thy loving-kindness in the morning, and Thy faithfulness every night, upon an instrument of ten strings, and upon the psaltery; upon the harp with a solemn sound. For Thou, LORD, hast made me glad through Thy works; I will triumph in the works of Thy Hands.

KJV

A WORD FROM ME: It is an awesome thing to give thanks to the LORD, for He is so good to us that there are not enough words to express the gratitude of our heart. This Psalm is written for the Sabbath day and is to be the center-point of worship. History says that this Psalm was dedicated to the Tribe of Judah by Moses. It is interesting that the center-piece of worship in the Temple and in the Sabbaths to come, is this Psalm dedicated to the Tribe of Judah. It is interesting because JESUS was of the Tribe of Judah, through both His Mother and His earthly Father, Joseph. It is interesting because all worship and praise belongs to JESUS and every knee shall bow in heaven and in the earth at His Name.

We sing praises in the early morning, as the sun rises to drive out the darkness of night. We herald the dawn by our thankfulness for the loving-kindness of GOD. We remember the Kindness, Mercy and Grace of GOD at the beginning of a new day, so that the overflow of the Love of GOD will carry us through every hour, showering us with blessings from His Sacred Heart. In the night we remember the faithfulness of GOD through the day that is past. Our heart overflows with thanksgiving for His Presence and His abundant shower of Goodness.

When we can't articulate our great love for GOD, we have the stringed instruments to sound forth His praises. The glorious sound of the majestic instruments, with harmonics that reach the heaven, carry the sound of our thanksgiving on wings to the very Throne of GOD. It is a language born on sound; giving eternal depth to our thanksgiving.

When I think of all the acts of Love that our Father accomplished for our salvation; that He gave His only Son so that we might live with Him, I cannot stop the song of continuous praise and thanks. All of the Trinity combined in bridging the gap between GOD and us. HOW CAN WE GIVE THANKS FOR ALL THAT HE HAS DONE? We can honor Him and praise Him; giving our heart to Him as a living sacrifice.

PSALM 93

The LORD reigneth; He is clothed with majesty. The LORD is clothed with strength, wherewith He hath girded Himself; the world also is established, that it cannot be moved. Thy Throne is established of old; Thou art from everlasting. The floods have lifted up, O LORD, the floods have lifted up their voice; the floods lift up their waves. The LORD on high is mightier than the noise of many waters, yea, than the mighty waves of the sea. Thy testimonies are very sure; holiness becometh Thine house, O LORD, forever.

KJV

A WORD FROM ME: I wrote the whole Psalm for us to read, because it says so very much in a few words.

This is the continuation of the Messianic Psalm 92 and it is dedicated, by Moses, to the Tribe of Benjamin, because "Benjamin never compromised his posture of Jewish pride in the face of enemies." We need to look at this Psalm through the lens of the Christian and declare THE LORD REIGNETH!!!!

Oftentimes, in the middle of the flood and waves of trouble, we forget that the "LORD is clothed with strength, wherewith He hath girded Himself; the world also is established, that it cannot be moved." Trouble tends to draw our eye toward it, and where our eye goes, so goes our heart. The result of looking at the waves and the flood is that we sink into the spirit of fear. This is what happened to Peter, who walked on the water while he was looking at JESUS, but sank when he looked at the storm. We need to take a page from Benjamin's book and stand firm in the face of the enemy. "The LORD on high is mightier than the noise of many waters, yea, than the might waves of the sea."

The LORD JESUS has bought our salvation with His precious Blood, we are safe in Him. "Thy testimonies are very sure; holiness becometh Thine house, O LORD, forever." "Forever" means without end. The LORD JESUS has testified, with His life, that the LORD GOD is from everlasting to everlasting and has established His Throne before the earth was created. Life in JESUS is firmly established in strength; but most of all, in unconditional love. BELOVED, WE ARE LOVED BY GOD.

PSALM 94:14, 15

For the LORD will not cast off His people, neither will He forsake His inheritance. But judgment shall return unto righteousness, and all the upright in heart shall follow it.

KJV

A WORD FROM ME: This is the fifth of the Psalms of Moses and it is dedicated to the Tribe of Gad. It is said that Elijah descended from this tribe. The tribe of Gad was renowned for its military strength and its ability to punish the attacking enemy. Elijah heralded the advent of the Messiah, JESUS, whose judgment is love.

This is a Psalm of good news for Israel and Christians throughout the world. "The LORD will not cast off His people, neither will He forsake His inheritance," this is the promise of GOD. Many will rise up against the people of GOD and seek to kill, steal and destroy the Nations who trust in GOD. Many will try to uproot the true vine, which is planted by the river of life; but GOD protects His vineyard. Thousands shall rise up, shouting death; GOD will arise and declare life.

When the judgment of GOD is realized, and nations repent of their sin against Him; when the hearts of man turn from wickedness, the GOD of unconditional love will arise and heal, restore and forgive. He will arise and protect His inheritance and those who follow Him, will be justified.

JESUS came that we might have life and life abundant in Him. His Blood reconciled us to GOD and we are His inheritance. We will never be forsaken, if we follow JESUS. The world is being shaken by wars and rumors of war; pestilence; fire; flood; earthquake; and storms. Drought threatens our food supply and man, in his wisdom cannot stop the shaking. People are shouting, "Help" and they fight to find answers to the shaking of the earth, but the only answer is found in JESUS, the Christ; He is the way, the truth and the life. Come to Him and be safe under the shadow of the Almighty.

> *If My people, who are called by my Name, shall humble themselves and pray and seek My face and turn from their wicked ways; then will I hear from Heaven and forgive their sin and heal their land.*
>
> 2 CHRONICLES 7:14 NIV

PSALM 95:1-8

Come, let us sing unto the LORD; let us make a joyful noise to the Rock of our salvation. Let us come before His presence with thanksgiving, and make a joyful noise unto Him with psalms. For the LORD is a great GOD and a great King above all gods. In His hand are the deep places of the earth; the strength of the hills is His also. The sea is His, and He made it and His hands formed the dry land. Oh, come, let us worship and bow down; let us kneel before the LORD our maker. For He is our GOD, and we are the people of His pasture, and the sheep of His hand; today if ye will hear His voice, harden not your heart, as in the day of provocation, and in the day of temptation in the wilderness.

KJV

A WORD FROM ME: This is the sixth Psalm of Moses and it is dedicated to the Tribe of Issachar. This tribe was known for its devotion to scholarly study of the Torah.

This Psalm is sung or chanted in every Morning Worship in the liturgical Churches. "Come," you are welcome, come into the presence of the LORD GOD who is your creator and maker; redeemer, Shepherd and friend. "Come" kneel before Him; worship and bow down. He, alone, is worthy of praise and worship; he is our GOD, JESUS is the Rock of our Salvation.

The quote from the Commentary inspires me to "sing the song" of the study of Scripture. It is a song that goes deep into the heart and continues to sing throughout our life. It is the song of GOD to our heart.

We are living in a time of uncertainty and confusion; like a wilderness filled with dark shadows. When we sing the song of the LORD in our heart, we will drive away all that darkness, that shadow of death, and the joy of the LORD will be our strength. Let us pray that all people will "strive for spiritual excellence and ecstasy and sing joyously unto GOD."

While we are living in the time of freedom and liberty in our Country, let us use this time to build up all those whom we know in the most Holy Faith, so that when the time of dryness and temptation comes, we will all, in one accord, sing the song of Holy Scripture unto the LORD, with great thanksgiving.

Your Thoughts:

PSALM 96:11-13

Let the heavens rejoice, and let the earth be glad; let the sea roar, and the fullness thereof. Let the field be joyful, and all that is therein, then shall all the trees of the forest rejoice before the LORD; for He cometh, for He cometh to judge the earth; He shall judge the world with righteousness, and the peoples with His truth.

KJV

A WORD FROM ME: It is said that historians do not really know to what Tribe of Israel that Moses dedicated this Psalm. However, some attempt to identify the tribe as being that of Zebulun. It is said that Zebulun supported his brother Issachar, who studied Torah continually.

We are living in that time spoken about by historians and proclaimed by Moses in this Psalm. JESUS fulfilled all the "predictions of the prophets" and "their prophecies concerning the redemption of Israel" was and is being fulfilled by JESUS. We are living in the age of the faith community that proclaims the belief in the "One and Only GOD Who created heaven and earth and Who controls nature and history".

Psalm 96 gives instruction to us, the community of faith in the One and Only GOD, it says: Sing unto the LORD; Declare His glory; Give to the LORD; and Worship the LORD. If we would follow these simple steps of honoring the LORD GOD, we would see His salvation and redemption, visible to those who have their eyes open, their ears attentive to His word, and their heart soft to receive His instruction and blessing.

We are living in prosperity when we live in the Lord. Count your blessings and give thanks that the lord is fulfilling his promises. Those promises of old are new every day in our life. We are living in the prosperity of the family of God - look around and look in your hand give thanks for all that He has provided for us.

PSALM 97:1, 2

The LORD reigneth; let the earth rejoice; let the multitude of isles be glad. Clouds and darkness are round about Him; righteousness and justice are the habitation of His Throne.

A WORD FROM ME: This is the eighth psalm of Moses, which corresponds to the blessings of the Tribes by the LORD recorded in Deuteronomy 33. According to Ibn Yachya, this psalm is dedicated to the Tribe of Joseph, composed of Ephraim and Manasseh. The Blessing of Moses on this tribe is found in Deuteronomy 33: 13-17, "Blessed of the LORD be his land...

In the Hebrew, the translation is: "When HASHEM will reign, the earth will exult; numerous islands will be glad". In the King James, it says that the "LORD reigns". This indicates to me that the post-JESUS translators have the understanding that the LORD is enthroned and reigns over all things; whereas the Hebrew understanding is that the LORD will reign. This is a strong contrast between those who "look for the coming of the Messiah" and those who "rejoice that the Messiah has come".

JESUS came and revealed to us that His Father reigns supreme over all the earth, and that all things in heaven and in the earth are His; He is LORD over them. JESUS is Messiah and thus, the earth is His and the earth and the "multitude of the isles" are glad.

I must ask a question that may startle some of you: Do you believe that the LORD will reign, at a time in the future? Or do you believe that the LORD reigns now and has dominion over all the earth, NOW? It makes a difference in how you look at the world around you and the things that happen in our world. What is your world view?

I will share with you of what my "world view" consists. I believe that JESUS redeemed this world by His willing sacrifice of Himself out of His great Love for His Father and for the world. JESUS is now enthroned in heaven, watching over this world that He loves so much. He grieves over the destruction, poverty, war, turmoil, arrogance and selfishness of the people; he is heart-sick over the lack of regard for human life. BUT GOD reigns and He sees the thick darkness that covers this earth. Isaiah called it "gross darkness" and it is gross.

In the midst of this "gross darkness", there shines a light. That Light comes directly from the LORD, who is the Light of the world. We are the lanterns that are illuminated by the Holy Spirit and we shine as a reflection of JESUS. We cannot overcome all the darkness in this world, but we can shine in our part of it. We have been set on fire by the Holy Spirit, now it is our responsibility to shine, keeping our lamps clean and burning. We are not to hide our lamp under a covering, so that the world cannot see the light, but we are to put it on a lamp stand so that all the people around us see, the Light of JESUS. We are His witnesses and our speech, conduct and actions should reflect the character of JESUS who reigns with the Father and the Holy Spirit, One GOD, world without end. OUR GOD REIGNS!!

PSALM 98:1

Oh, sing unto the LORD a new song; for He hath done marvelous things; His right hand, and His holy Arm, have gotten Him the victory.

A WORD FROM ME: This Psalm is dedicated by Moses to the Tribe of Naftali.

The Midrash Tanchuma lists ten great songs of faith which highlight Jewish history. This Psalm is considered the 10th and last. It is the song of the Messiah. The ten songs are:

1. The song the Jews sang on the first night of Passover when they were redeemed from Egypt;
2. The Song of the Sea, when GOD parted the Red Sea (Exodus 15: 1-21);
3. The song dedicated to Miriam's well (Numbers 21: 17-20)
4. Moses' final song before His death (Deuteronomy 32);

5. Joshua's song of victory (Joshua 10:12);
6. Deborah's song of victory (Judges 5);
7. David's song of salvation from his enemies (II Samuel, 22 and Psalm 18);
8. David's song for the inauguration of the Temple (Psalm 30);
9. King Solomon's Song of Songs;
10. This Psalm, Psalm 98.

It is said that, "In the redemption of the future, GOD will act with both the Hand and the Arm of salvation, for all the power will emanate from GOD'S mercy, regardless of *merits*." The right hand of GOD is the hand of strength, power and is governed by love and mercy. It is true that Love and mercy will gain the victory over all things evil. We must take this seriously; having our life sing the song of love, mercy and compassion.

It is very interesting that the Born-again Children of the Living GOD know one another by the Spirit that is within them; the Spirit of GOD. This Spirit manifests itself in the beautiful song of the redeemed which the soul sings. The NEW SONG is the song of the heart that loves JESUS. Could it be that He and the entire heavenly host sing this song with the redeemed of the earth?

SING, DEAR SISTERS AND BROTHERS THE HEAVENLY SONG OF LOVE AND MERCY, UNTIL THE WHOLE EARTH IS FILLED WITH THE SONG OF GOD.

PSALM 99:5

Exalt ye the LORD our GOD, and worship at his footstool;
FOR HE IS HOLY.

KJV

A WORD FROM ME: This Psalm is dedicated by Moses to the tribe of Dan (Iban Yachya).

FOR HE IS HOLY, HIS NAME IS HOLY, THE LORD OUR GOD IS HOLY.

I want to stress the fact that the LORD our GOD is Holy and every part of Him, is Holy. Yes, He is our Father; He is Abba, Daddy; He is our friend; He is our portion; He is our healer; He sustains us; He delivers us; He redeems our life from destruction; but do not forget, when you approach the LORD, HE IS HOLY.

The Holy One deserves are adoration, worship, devotion and our whole being yielded to Him. He is the most trustworthy, the song goes, "I know whom I have believed and am persuaded that He is able to keep that which I've committed unto Him, against that day." There is no one more trustworthy than the LORD GOD. All others will fail in the course of life, BUT GOD will never fail; His love will never become cool or cold; He is always passionately in love with His children.

When we worship the LORD, exalt his Name and praise Him, we should do so in the deepest reverence of our heart. He is our Daddy, friend, Father, and great companion of our soul, but familiarity with Him does not mean that He is to be acknowledged in a casual manner; HE IS HOLY, HIS NAME IS HOLY, and FOR THE LORD GOD IS THE HOLY ONE.

We are always welcome to come into His courts with praise; we are always welcome to come to the Throne of Grace and Mercy; we are always welcome to bring our whole self to Him for healing and wholeness; we are always welcome. We are welcome because JESUS paid the price for us to come boldly to the throne of Grace and Mercy. It is through His Blood that we are made worthy to enter into His presence. It cost GOD His highest and His best so that we might have life; He paid it all, we are the recipients of so great a gift that there are not words to say "thank you". Another song says, "What shall I give Him, poor as I am; if I were a shepherd, I would give a lamb; if I were a wise man, I would do my part; what I have I give Him, GIVE MY HEART" Yes, what we have, we can give Him, give our heart.

PSALM 100

Make a joyful noise unto the LORD, all ye lands. Serve the LORD with gladness; come before His presence with singing. Know ye that the LORD, He is GOD; it is He who has made us, and not we our selves; we are His people, and the sheep of His pasture. Enter into His gates with thanksgiving, and into His courts with praise; be thankful unto Him, and bless His Name. For the LORD is good, His mercy is everlasting, and His truth endureth to all generations.

KJV

A WORD FROM ME: Ibn Yachya says that Moses dedicated this psalm to the tribe of Asher, whom he blessed with special bounty. (Deuteronomy 33: 24) This Psalm is sung during the Thank offering service in the Temple and is sung in the Thanksgiving services in the Church. What are we thankful for in this life? COUNT YOUR BLESSINGS AND NAME THEM ONE BY ONE; IT WILL SURPRISE YOU WHAT THE LORD HAS DONE FOR YOU. Do you feel the blessing of GOD right now?

The goodness of the LORD endures forever; He is goodness; He is mercy; He is love and we are the recipients of all that He has in His storehouse. This should set out feet-a-dancing and a song in our heart all day long. Our Father desires the very best for us and He showed it by giving His Son for the redemption of the world. WE ARE LIVING IN THE PROSPERITY OF THE BLESSING OF GOD. We should never stop thanking Him for all that He has done for us.

When we enter into His presence, His presence is always with us, we should shout with praise and bless His Name. He made us into His image and gave us a heart to be yielded unto Him as an offering of thanksgiving. "Nothing in our hands we bring; simply to Thy cross we cling." What a privilege to call the LORD GOD, OUR FATHER, Blessed be He.

This ends the Psalms of Moses, found by David and incorporated into the Biblical Psalms. All of these Psalms, 90-100 are known a Messianic Age Psalms, because they point to the Messiah. JESUS, the only begotten Son of the Living GOD, is our Messiah and to Him be all glory, honor and praise.

YOUR THOUGHTS:

PSALM 101:1

I will sing of mercy and judgment; unto Thee, O LORD, will I sing.

KJV

A WORD FROM ME: This is a psalm of David, where he proclaims that he will live a devout life unto GOD and strive for excellence in his living. David used his psalms to bring him close to GOD; he would meditate on the LORD through the vehicle of music.

Today, as I was cleaning my house, I was listening to soft, beautiful songs that were sung and played by excellent musicians. The music lifted me from the stress of cleaning, into the place of reverence. Before I knew it, the work was done and my heart was still singing. David was lifted from the stress of his life into the life of beauty in GOD. Through this "lifted" state, he heard the voice of GOD speaking softly in his heart, encouraging him to vow before GOD to "walk within my house with a perfect heart." (Verse 26)

What was the "house" of which David was speaking in verse 2? I believe that the "house" is the body that walks the path of the earthly life. David was saying that he would strive to keep his heart fixed on the LORD while he walked the path of life.

We, too, can make this commitment to GOD. While we live in this earthly house — our flesh - we will sing praises to GOD for all that He has done for us and strive to keep His ways with a fixed heart. This commitment sets my heart a-singing, because I know that this relationship with GOD, made possible by His unconditional love through JESUS Christ, makes Him well-pleased.

We were created to fellowship with GOD; worship Him in spirit and in truth. We were created to sing His mercy and praise among the people; an instrument of glory and praise of the Living GOD. We were created to inspire and encourage others to sing unto the LORD a beautiful song. We were created by GOD to be a well-tuned instrument of praise in a world that hovers in darkness. SING UNTO THE LORD, O PEOPLE OF GOD.

PSALM 102:16-18

When the LORD shall build up Zion, He shall appear in His glory. He will regard the prayer of the destitute, and not despise their prayer. This is written for the generation to come; and the people who shall be created shall praise the LORD.

KJV

A MESSIANIC PROPHECY

A WORD FROM ME: It is exciting to see this prophecy of the coming of JESUS in the generations following King David. JESUS was born in the lineage of David and David included in His Psalms many words of prophecy about the coming of the Son of GOD. This is one of them.

JESUS was born in the glory of GOD, humble, meek and lowly, yet mighty, strong and all powerful. This contrast is seen throughout the life of JESUS. He was gentle, kind and humble when He was with the people who were honest and sincere; He was mighty, strong and all powerful in His love of His Father and in meeting the needs of the poor. JESUS, the King of glory, did not exalt Himself; He humbled Himself, taking the form of a servant, He healed, restored and forgave, touching all people with His great Love.

We see, in JESUS a definition of power and strength that is uncommon in the world today. Power and strength, in the way of JESUS, is manifested in quiet confidence, humility of being and strength in devotion to His Father. It is through this power and strength that JESUS willingly yielded Himself to the horrible death on the cross. Why did He submit, when He could have called 12 legions of angels to deliver Him from the situation? Because, His love for His Father, His love for all creation and His obedience to the Mission of Redemption was stronger than His love of His own life. THAT IS THE POWER AND STRENGTH OF JESUS - HIS GLORY.

JESUS heard the prayer of the destitute and did not despise their prayers; instead, He healed, restored and prospered them and US with Eternal life. We are not used to being referred to as destitute and yet, the human race was destitute until the coming of JESUS. The word "destitute" means, empty of the way and ability to support oneself, impoverished. Without JESUS, humankind was empty of the way and means to come to the Throne of Grace and the Presence of GOD. JESUS bridged the gap between GOD and man by his own Blood offered for our salvation. JESUS took our poverty, in order to bestow eternal riches to all who come to Him.

Endless praise and thanksgiving belong to JESUS, who bore our poverty, despising the shame and trusted the Almighty

Power of His Father to raise Him from the dead to reign with Him in Glory. We too, will reign with Him forever; THANKS BE TO GOD.

PSALM 103:1-5

*Bless the Lord, O my soul: and all that is within me,
 bless his holy name.
Bless the Lord, O my soul, and forget not all his
 benefits:
Who forgiveth all thine iniquities; who healeth all thy
 diseases;
Who redeemeth thy life from destruction; who
 crowneth thee with lovingkindness and tender
 mercies;
Who satisfieth thy mouth with good things; so that thy
 youth is renewed like the eagle's.*

KJV

A WORD FROM ME: "When upon life's billows you are tempest tossed; when you are discouraged, thinking all is lost. Count your many blessings, name them one by one, and it will surprise you what the LORD has done." "Bless the LORD, O my soul, and all that is within me bless His Holy Name." When we enter into his courts with praise, we are surrounded with the light of the heavenly realm. No darkness can invade the Holy place of His presence. We enter into that Holy Place by giving our whole soul, and spirit to the LORD; yielding even our flesh to dwell in the Light of His Love. All is calm, all is bright, all is Holy, and all is beautiful in the presence of the LORD.

When we count the many blessings of the LORD we are amazed by the complete and perfect way in which He has surrounded us with His love. He forgives all our stumbling and missteps; He heals us from our dis-eases; He redeems us by His shed Blood; He gives us a crown of glory, we are free to enter into His presence; He provides for us in every way and renews our strength even in our old age. There is nothing that the LORD has not provided for us, His Children.

This time of remembering and giving thanks, let us not forget that every breath we take is a gift from GOD. Breathe in Christ and let Him fill every cell of your body with the glorious presence of the Living LORD; be filled with His Holy Spirit and mount up with wings like the eagle.

THANK YOU, JESUS.

PSALM 104

Thou sendest forth thy spirit, they are created: and thou renewest the face of the earth. The glory of the LORD shall endure for ever: the LORD shall rejoice in his works.He looketh on the earth, and it trembleth: he toucheth the hills, and they smoke.I will sing unto the LORD as long as I live: I will sing praise to my God while I have my being.My meditation of him shall be sweet: I will be glad in the LORD. Let the sinners be consumed out of the earth, and let the wicked be no more. Bless thou the LORD, O my soul. Praise ye the LORD.

KJV

A WORD FROM ME: The Psalm causes me to greatly rejoice in the Lord. He has done such great things out of His great love; He created beauty and order with a plan that all things would prosper.

Verse 24 says: "O Lord, how manifold are thy works! In wisdom hast thou made them all; the earth is full of Thy Riches."

Why did the Lord God do all of this for the earth? He revealed His very nature; a love that creates all things to thrive and be prosperous. His desire is that all things flourish.

The wicked have no place in the beautiful unfolding of the Love of God. Wickedness cannot love, only eat away at the beauty. When sinners repent, the Great Love of God restores the beauty and establishes the image of Love in the soul.

"Bless thou the Lord o my soul, Praise ye the Lord."

PSALM 105:14, 15

He permitted no man to do them wrong; yea, He reproved Kings for their sakes, saying, "Touch not Mine anointed, and do My prophets no harm."

KJV

A WORD FROM ME: This Psalm was written when the Ark of the Covenant was placed in the Temple in Jerusalem. Even today, this Psalm and Psalm 96 are part of the permanent Songs of the day with 105 in the morning and 96 in the evening.

There is a very deep meaning to these verses, which each of us should hold as precious. GOD is in control of everything and throughout all of history, He has stood guard over all His own. He never leaves, nor forsakes His children, they are never cast into the shadows to die in the dark. Instead, He permits no man to do them wrong; He reproves Kings for their sake. GOD stands up and declares with all authority and all power, "Touch not Mine anointed, and do My prophets no harm." These are the words of the LORD that He declares and stands on.

The question still remains; do you honor all of the anointed of GOD in the same way that GOD honors them? Do you understand that when you are filled with the Holy Spirit, you are anointed by GOD? Do you respect yourself as the Temple of the Holy Spirit with the LORD dwell ing in you? Do you understand that you are beloved of GOD and that He honors you? Therefore, if GOD thought so much about each of us and loved us unconditionally, should not we honor, love and serve one another, doing no harm, but respect the other as anointed children of the Living GOD.

Your Thoughts:

PSALM 106:7, 8

*Our Fathers understood not Thy wonders in Egypt;
they remembered not the multitude of Thy mercies,
but provoked Him at the sea, even at the Red Sea.
Nevertheless, He saved them for His name's sake,
that He might make His mighty power to be known.*

KJV

A WORD FROM ME: "Nevertheless, He saved them for His Name's sake". Think about those words and what they might mean to your life. GOD had made a Covenant with Israel; GOD kept His Word to them; Israel broke its Covenant with GOD, BUT GOD never broke Covenant with them - FOR HIS NAME SAKE.

When GOD puts his Name to a Covenant, He stands by it and never breaks it. GOD made a Covenant with man that was sealed with the precious Blood of JESUS; for His Holy Name Sake, He will never break that Covenant, it is sealed forever.

Read Ezekiel 36: 21-23. Verse 23 says: "I will sanctify My great Name, which was profaned among the nations, which you have profaned in the midst of them; and the nations shall know that I am the LORD, saith the LORD GOD, when I shall be sanctified in you before their eyes." His great mercy reached through the thick darkness of sin and, remembering His Covenant with Israel, redeemed them from destruction and made them a witness of His mercy.

Likewise, GOD sent his Son as redeemer of the world; He is our Re deemer, Savior and friend. It was His great Love for us that caused Him to sacrifice His Highest and his best for lost humankind. It is His Honor and faithfulness that stands strong for the world today.

Think about this: For whose sake do you live, move and have your be ing? For whose sake do you ask, seek and knock? Is it for your sake, or is it for His Holy Name Sake? Check your motives for asking, seeking and knocking, ask yourself for whose sake do you want deliverance, healing, strength and salvation. Is it to escape pain for yourself or an other, or is it to glorify GOD and serve Him. Is your relationship with GOD one of love, adoration, and worship or is it give me, give me, and give me what I want?

Remember the ten lepers, ten were healed, only one came back to give thanks to JESUS. The one who gave thanks, was the one who was made whole in mind, body and spirit. The one received, through faith in JESUS, a more prefect healing. In all things, give thanks to the LORD, for He is worthy to be praised.

PSALM 107:8

Oh, that men would praise the LORD for His goodness, and for His wonderful works to the children of men!

KJV

What can I give Him, poor as I am? If I were a shepherd, I would give a lamb; If I were a wise man, I would do my part; Yet what I can I give Him, GIVE MY HEART.

"IN THE BLEAK MID-WINTER" - CHRISTINA ROSSETTI

IN THE BLEAK mid-winter of the heart of man, JESUS comes as a lowly child, gentle, sweet, and filled with love. He is born in the darkness of the hard heart and brings the spark of light from

GOD. In the world around, the crowds are crushing and pushing; laughing and shouting; arguing and fighting, but the LORD JESUS comes in the stillness of the night, bringing Holy Light.

The simple, common man hears the singing of Angels who herald the birth in the secret place in the soul. They see the light and hasten to adore the newborn King. Wise men, looking for the Light, come with prophetic gifts for the King. All the while the gentle Light of JESUS is growing brighter in the soul of a new believer.

Around this new, precious soul are terrors and threats. The jealous Herod of the world and the covetous Pharisees hover around to destroy the Light in the new believer, but GOD guards and protects the soul from harm and the Light of JESUS grows brighter and stronger. Oh, that men would praise the LORD for His goodness, and for His wonderful works to the children of men!

"The people who walked in darkness have seen a great light; they that dwell in the land of the shadow of death, upon them hath the light shined." (Isaiah 9:2) "For unto us a child is born, unto us a son is given, and the government shall be upon His shoulders; and His Name shall be called Wonderful, Counselor, The Mighty GOD, The Everlasting Father, The Prince of Peace." (Isaiah 9: 6)

Oh, that men would praise the LORD for His goodness, and for His wonderful works to the children of men!

PSALM 108:1-6

O GOD, my heart is fixed; I will sing and give praise, even with my glory. Awake, psaltery and harp; I myself will awake early. I will praise Thee, O LORD, among the peoples; and I will sing praises unto Thee among the nations; for Thy mercy is great above the heavens, and Thy truth reacheth unto the clouds. Be Thou exalted, O GOD, above the heavens, and Thy glory above all the earth. That Thy beloved may be delivered, save with Thy right hand, and answer me.

KJV

A WORD FROM ME: Do you notice that King David refers to himself as "beloved"? Do you understand that you are "beloved of GOD"? Just think what that means, to be "beloved of GOD" Yes, you and I are so precious to GOD that he gave his only Son to be born, live, suffer and die for you, so that you could live with Him forever. He loved you so much that He gave you the choice of life or death and urged, strongly that you choose life; He did not choose for you, you have the choice. You are His beloved, He loves you.

My testimony is, "O GOD, my heart is fixed; I will sing and give praise...I will praise Thee, O LORD, among the peoples; and I will sing praises unto Thee among the nations." Jeremiah speaks of GOD in this way, "It is because of the LORD'S mercies that we are not consumed, because His compassions fail not, they are new every morning; great is Thy faithfulness. The LORD is my portion, saith my soul; therefore will I hope in Him."

We are at the dawn of a new year, and yet, the mercy and compassion of the LORD is new every day. When we awake, He is there with a fresh, new anointing of mercy and compassion. So, dear ones, "Awake, psaltery and harp... awake early...for His mercy is great above the heavens and His truth reaches unto the clouds. Be Thou exalted, O GOD, above the heavens, and Thy glory above all the earth." Praise the LORD with all your heart from the rising of the sun to its setting. Let your life radiate the mercy and compassion of GOD throughout the day and when the night comes, let His Light be your light in the darkness.

PSALM 109:1-4

Hold not thy peace, O God of my praise; For the mouth of the wicked and the mouth of the deceitful are opened against me: they have spoken against me with a lying tongue. They compassed me about also with words of hatred; and fought against me without a cause. For my love they are my adversaries: but I give myself unto prayer.

KJV

A WORD FROM ME: Notice how many times the word mouth, words and spoken are used. The mouth contains a tongue that forms words to be spoken. It is written "out of the abundance of the heart, the mouth speaks." A wicked heart and wicked thoughts spill over into the mouth. The tongue gives words to the thoughts which come from the heart, and the spoken word can kill the hearer.

David gives an answer to the dilemma of how to stop the

wicked thoughts, mouth, words and speech. He says: "but I give myself unto prayer." The Hebrew says: "But I am prayer."

David always turned to the Lord God, therefore, he became a "living prayer".

This tells me that if I live a lifestyle of prayer to the Lord God and all things evoke prayer in my heart, then out of my heart flows words of Hope.

PSALM 110:1-4

The LORD said unto my LORD, "Sit Thou at My right hand, until I make Thine enemies Thy footstool". The LORD shall send the rod of Thy strength out of Zion; rule Thou in the midst of Thine enemies. Thy people shall be willing in the day of Thy power; in the beauties of holiness from the womb of the morning, Thou hast the dew of Thy youth. The LORD hath sworn, and will not repent, "Thou art a priest forever after the order of Melchizedek"

KJV

A WORD FROM ME: This is one of the strongest of the Messianic Psalms and points to JESUS in every verse.

1. It affirms the Deity of JESUS;
2. It proclaims the eternal priesthood of JESUS, as Priest according to the Order of Melchizedek;

3. It begins with the ascension of JESUS and looks into the future;
4. It is a prophecy of the time when JESUS will come again in power as deliverer.

When JESUS comes again in glory, people will see and bow down and bend the knee; they will worship Him in the beauty of Holiness. The enemy of GOD will be under His feet and will not hurt or harm anymore. This is the coming of the King-Priest, who will gather the faithful to Himself as His loyal children.

Holiness is beautiful; Holiness is lovely; Holiness is right and righteous with GOD. We can seek and find that beauty, and righteousness in our life, right now. As we begin a new calendar year, let us seek and find the path of Holiness that is found in JESUS Christ the LORD. Let us walk in that path and grow in grace and the love and knowledge of JESUS. Take your Scripture and read, study and inwardly digest the Word of Truth, then apply it to your own life. I see Holiness as another word for the "fixed heart" of Psalm 108: 1. When your heart if fixed on the LORD and your eye is turned to JESUS in all things, then you will find that the path of Holiness is a path that is beautiful, and lovely, because it is righteous.

The way of the world is dark and gloomy, there is no light except the artificial light of light bulbs. Look to the Light of Christ and be filled with His glorious Light and walk in it. When you do this, the world around will be enlightened by the LORD and, as the song goes, "It only takes a spark to set a fire going; and soon all those around will warm up to its glowing. That's how it is with GOD'S Love."

Your Thoughts:

PSALM 111:1, 2, 8-10

Praise ye the LORD, I will praise the LORD with my whole heart, in the assembly of the upright, and in the congregation. The works of the LORD are great, sought out of all them who have pleasure therein... They stand fast forever and ever, and are done in truth and uprightness. He sent redemption unto His people; He hath commanded His Covenant forever; Holy and reverend is His Name. The fear of the LORD is the beginning of wisdom. A good understanding have all they that do His commandments; His praise endureth forever.

KJV

A WORD FROM ME: I noticed in the first verse of this Psalm, a distinction between the "assembly of the upright and the congregation". When you see a distinction, through the use of words, you need to look into it. The "assembly of the upright," according to the Hebrew understanding, is composed of those who are wise and scholarly in the Word of the LORD, these are your teachers and preachers of the Word. The "Congregation" is composed of the hearers of the Word and those who grow through the teaching and preaching. What is very clear in this first verse is that praise of the LORD is to be voiced and lived in and among those who are learned and those who are in need of understanding. Praise of the LORD is never to be withheld from anyone.

"With my whole heart" reminds me of the verse in Deuteronomy 6: 5, which is a command from the LORD: "Thou shalt love the LORD thy GOD with all thine heart, and with all thy soul, and with all thy might." And JESUS added, from Leviticus 19: 18, "Thou shalt love thy neighbor as thyself; I Am the LORD." This is the commandment of the LORD, wholehearted love of the LORD and the neighbor; no exceptions. The Psalm goes on to talk about the "works of the LORD". They are great, honorable, glorious, wonderful, memorable, and stand fast for ever and ever. The "works of the LORD are done in truth and uprightness" and "verity and justice." The works of the LORD endure forever and ever. The works of ours, apart from the LORD, are filthy rags, mixed with uncleanness; the Works of the LORD are pure and righteous al together. Therefore, we must stand in the LORD's presence and receive from His Hand the direction for anything that we do. Prayer and the study of the Holy Scripture will fix our heart and mind on Him and we must love Him with all our heart, soul, mind and might and love our neighbor as ourselves.

Verse 9 speaks of the Redemption that we have received from the LORD through the willing sacrifice of JESUS, the Word of GOD made flesh. The Blood of JESUS reconciles us to GOD, therefore we can stand in His presence and receive from

His Hand as children of the Living GOD. He has commanded His Covenant, sealed with the Blood of JESUS; Holy and reverend is His Name, the Name above all Names. The Book of Proverbs often quotes verse 10: "The fear of the LORD is the beginning of wisdom." The Psalm goes on to say, that those who keep the commandments of GOD and do them have good under standing of the Word of the LORD. Teachers and preachers must never withhold this understanding from any of those who hear them. The praise of the LORD shall continually be in our mouth.

PSALM 112

*Praise ye the Lord, Blessed is the man who feareth the
Lord who delighteth greatly in his commandments.
His seed shall be mighty upon the earth the Generation
of the upright shall be Blessed.
He shall not be afraid of evil tidings; His heart is fixed
trusting in the Lord
His Heart is established; he shall not be afraid, until he
sees his desire upon His enemies.*

KJV

A WORD FROM ME: David begins this Psalm with praise and with a statement of Blessing. The Psalm establishes the reader in an attitude of worship.

I am drawn to the fact that when we fix our hearts on Praise of the LORD and the Blessing of others, all else seems to be less significant. The dark side of life gives way to the light of the Glory of GOD.

David goes on to say that the generations of a "man who fears the LORD" shall be mighty and blessed. This is a prophetic Word from the heart of GOD through David. For JESUS, the Son of GOD, was and is mighty to save those who follow Him and are upright in their relation to others.

David goes on to say that his heart is fixed on the LORD GOD, he trusts the LORD; therefore he has no fear of evil tidings or what man can do to him.

I wonder what could happen to our entire life, if we could fix our heart on the LORD GOD and trust in Him completely? David did; so should we. The result is peace.

PSALM 113:1-3

*Praise ye the LORD! Praise, O ye servants of the
    LORD, Praise the Name of the LORD.
Blessed be the Name of the LORD from this time forth
    and forever more.
From the rising of the son unto the going down of the
    same, the LORD's name is to be praised.*

KJV

A WORD FROM ME: Psalms 11 through 13 and 115-117 are called Hallelujah Psalms. They are a celebration of Life that lives in Praise of the Living GOD. Praise cancels out darkness, gloom and evil, because the Glory of Praise transcends conditions and unveils the Presence of GOD.

I want to focus on the Power of the Name of the LORD. It is the Name above all names. What can be named is below the Name of GOD. His Name is Holy. His Name created all things. His name surpasses all things.

The devout people will only say His name in a Holy manner; for the LORD GOD is worthy of great and glorious praise. The devout people call Him Hashem or Adonai or Jehovah. YHWH is pure breath, the great breath that breathed life into all things. (Genesis 2:7) The breath of life was breathed into man and he "became a living soul".

It is understood that with Heth and Van GOD breathed life. These are the basic letters of the Holy Name. Let us remember the Name of the Lord and our GOD (Psalm 20:7).

The Holy Name creates life; Praise His name!!! What is your "desire upon your enemies"? Do you pray for their harm? Or do you pray for their good? JESUS prayed "Father forgive them; for they know not what they do." (Luke 23 :34) He prayed forgiveness for those that crucified Him. How, then, can we refuse to grant forgiveness to those who hurt us!!!

PSALM 114:7,8

*Tremble, O earth, at the presence of the God of Jacob
who turned the rock into a pool, the hard rock into
springs of water.*

NIV

THINK ABOUT IT: The Lord God, who made all things in the heavens and on earth, has the power to re-create, heal or to terminate. A potter has in his hands the ability to make a pot or to remake a pot or to crumble what is made into a ball of clay again. God is the potter and we are the clay. All the earth is dependent on the will of the Divine Potter.

The earth knows the power of the Creator; it knows that it is dependent on the love that the Creator has for it. We see the trees clapping their hands as the wind blows through the leaves. We see how the earth comes into bloom when watered by rain. We see the glory of the Lord revealed in the heavens by day and by night. We see how the seas ebb and flow by the design of the

Creator. We see all this with our human eye sight and rest in the knowledge that the Creator has all things under His control.

The earth trembles in the awe of the majesty of God at the awesome presence of the Lord.

My question is: Do we tremble at the fact that this Potter, the Lord God, loves each of us, whom He created. So much, that He gave His only Son, Jesus to redeem the broken world filled of marred pots?

Think about it!!

PSALM 115:1, 16-18

A Hallelujah Psalm

> *Not to us, Lord, not to us but to your name be the glory, because of your love and faithfulness. The highest heavens belong to the LORD, but the earth he has given to mankind. It is not the dead who praise the LORD, those who go down to the place of silence; it is we who extol the LORD, both now and forevermore.*
>
> NIV

Think about it: Psalm 114 speaks about the power of Creator God and that the earth trembles at the presence of the Lord.

Psalm 115 reminds us that the glory belongs to the Lord, not to us. The heavens belong to the Lord and the earth has been given to man, to tend and keep.

It reminds me of the landowner who went on a trip and gave the land he owned to his workman. He expected the workman to care for his property. It is the Lord God who expects us to care for the gift of this earth with the same love that He has for it.

Our praise and honor of the Lord; our thanksgiving for the riches He has given to us, makes a difference in His heart. Could it be that our care for Him, our honor and praise of Him is our greatest ministry to Him? Could it be that our love, care and honor of others is the joy that blesses His heart?

Let us extol the Lord both now and forever.

PSALM 116:12-14

How can I repay the Lord for all His goodness to me? I will lift up the cup of salvation and call on the name of the LORD. I will fulfill my vows to the LORD in the presence of all his people.

NIV

THINK ABOUT IT: Wow! The question asked in verse 12 is one that I hear from people who are overwhelmed with gratitude for what the Lord has done for them. "How can I repay the Lord for all His goodness to me?"

David offers two ways in which he will thank the Lord for his goodness. One is to: lift up the cup of salvation and call upon the name of the Lord; The second is that he will fulfill and be faithful to the vows he has made to the Lord so that others will see and be encouraged to follow. One was for himself that from his heart, he will extol the Lord, the other is that his behavior will inspire others to glorify God.

David has provided us with two ideas for glorifying God, I am sure there are other ways. I encourage you to make a list of your ways to answer that profound question: How can I repay the Lord for all His goodness to me?

Write your thoughts:

PSALM 117:1,2

Praise the LORD, all you nations; extol him, all you peoples. For great is his love toward us, and the faithfulness of the LORD endures forever. Praise the LORD.

NIV

A WORD FROM ME: This Psalm calls for all people to praise the Lord and extol His name. It is a fact that all people do not praise Him and glorify Him. It is a fact that a large number of people do not know the love of God for them, nor do they know that He is faithful.

What are we going to do about it? Yes, we can pray and we can act. We can show the love of Jesus by being an instrument of His love to others. We can show His faithfulness by being faithful in our relationship with others. We can show that God is trustworthy by being trustworthy in our relationship with others. By our life we can witness to the glory of the Most High God and extol His name among the people.

Write down your ideas, then make a plan to fulfill those ideas.

PSALM 118:6-9

The Lord is on my side; I will not fear. What can man do to me? The Lord is for me among those who help me;
Therefore I shall see my desire on those who hate me. It is better to trust in the Lord than to put confidence in man. It is better to trust in the Lord than to put confidence in princes.

NKJV

A WORD FROM ME: At the beginning of this Psalm are the words: "Give thanks to the LORD for He is good; His mercy (Kindness) endures forever." This is a general thanks to GOD, to be repeated often by all people. "No matter what occurs, GOD is always good and everything He does is for the best, even though this may not be immediately apparent to man". In everything give thanks to GOD is taught and understood by most Christians, however, it is a concept that is hard to enact when the troubles of life encompass you about. Psalm 118 is a Psalm for times of distress.

Verses 6-9 are words of encouragement to all of us and echo the words of JESUS who said, "Fear Not". When we take refuge in the LORD there is no reason to fear anything; "how can man affect me?" When we rely on GOD for our support and strength, we are placing our trust in the One who is always faithful, who has our best interest at heart. He is our strong tower, our fortress, our deliverer and our best friend; ABBA Father.

As we begin a new year, we may have areas of our life that trouble us greatly. Don't bring that baggage into the new days ahead. Empty your life of the burdens of the past and go forward in GOD, sheltered under the Almighty Wing of the great I AM. Have no fear, for HASHEM is with you.

On another note: we allow things to affect us . We have control over the things that bring us up or down, emotionally and psychologically. This is why GOD says, "Choose this day whom you will serve; GOD or mammon." The choice is ours, Psalm 118: 8, 9 says that it is better to take refuge in GOD than to rely on man or nobles. GOD IS FOREVER FAITHFUL AND WILL GIVE YOU THE HIGHEST AND THE BEST. TRUST HIM!!!

PSALM 119:105

Your word is a lamp for my feet and a light for my path.

JPS TANAKH 1917

A WORD FROM ME: This is the first verse under the Hebrew alphabet letter - NUN. I decided to do a study on the Hebrew Alphabet and the meanings of each letter, since this Psalm is based on the Alphabet and each line of the stanzas of 8 verses begins with the alphabet sequence. When you know the meaning of the Hebrew letter, you can uncover, more readily, the deeper meaning of the 8 verses.

HEBREW ALPHABET AND THE MEANING OF EACH LETTER:

1. Aleph - means the head.
2. Beis - means to understand.
3. Gimel - means to do kindness to others.

4. Delet - means the doorway. *When you put gimel and delet together it means that doing kindness, is the door or the way to the path of truth.*
5. Heh - the narrow way. It stands for the Holy Name of GOD and with vav, GOD created everything that is.
6. Vav - means Truth. Truth leads to harmony and unity; false hood leads to dissension and strife.
7. Zayin - means remember.
8. Ches - means Grace; the gift from following GOD.
9. Tes - means goodness; the blessing of goodness comes when all the letters above are fulfilled.
10. Yud - means inheritance, the humility of God, the inheritance of the people of God and it also means littleness. The world was created with the smallest of the letters. This is the first letter in the name "Jesus."
11. Chaf - means the palm of the hand. Scripture says that we are written on the palm of the hand of GOD.
12. Lamed - means the study of scripture and represents the "heart." Remember, "Thy word have I hid in my heart that I might not sin against Thee." The deeper meaning of that verse is that the study of the Word of GOD keeps us focused on what is righteous with GOD.
13. Mem - means speak the Word. It is part of the English word, "remember."
14. Nun - means loyal and devoted to GOD. The Lamp of GOD's Word enlightens the soul.
15. Samach - means to support. GOD supports all those who rely on Him.
16. Ayin - means the poor. With samach it means that man's duty is to support the poor. This is the root

meaning of "poor in spirit." Poverty can be revealed by looking and seeing it.
17. Peh - means mouth. With Ayin it means that the eye should study the Scripture before the mouth speaks a word.
18. Tzaddi - means submission to GOD.
19. Kuf - means sanctity. Strive to repent and receive GOD's assistance.
20. Resh - means wicked. The wicked are so arrogant that they put themselves ahead of others.
21. Shin - means falsehood. "falsehood does not have feet." It cannot travel unless it is carried by an agent.
22. Tov - means truth. It is the final word of GOD. The Seal of GOD is Truth.

As you study Psalm 119, be aware that GOD has given to you His deep Word so that you will grow in grace and the love and knowledge of Him. His Word is a lamp unto your feet and a light unto your path.

PSALM 119:155,156,160,163, 164,169,175,176

Resh - wicked
Deliverance is far from the wicked, for they do not study Your statutes. Great is Your compassion, O LORD; preserve my life, according to Your judgments... The heart of Your word is truth; all Your righteous judgments endure for evermore.

Shin - sin — falsehood
As for lies, I hate and abhor them, but Your law is my love. Seven times a day do I praise You, because of Your righteous judgments.

Tav - truth
Let my cry come before you, O LORD; give me understanding, according to Your word...Let me live, and I will praise You, and let your judgments help me. I have gone astray, like a sheep that is lost;

search for Your servant, for I do not forget Your commandments.

A WORD FROM ME: The last three letters of the Hebrew Alphabet are: resh, shin and tav. These last three, carry a very important meaning.

Resh means wicked. The study of the Holy Scripture is the source of truth; therefore, to avoid living out the meaning of "resh" a person should be in the Word of GOD daily.

Shin (sin) means falsehood. The Psalmist declares that he hates and abhors lies, so he gives his attention to the Word of GOD.

Tav means truth. Tav is the last letter in the Hebrew Alphabet and declares that the last word of GOD is truth. "Truth is the final and ultimate purpose of all pursuits and action — the seal of GOD Himself is truth. The man who finds truth will also find the path which leads to GOD." (Talmud)

When Jesus stood before Pilate he said: "To this end was I born, and for this cause came I into the world, that I should bear witness unto the truth. Everyone that is of the truth heareth my voice." Pilate said: "What is truth?". Standing before Pilate, was Truth Himself. Jesus is Truth. He said: "I am the way, the truth and the life." If anyone seeks the truth, it will be found in Jesus, who is eternal truth.

GOD has given us the way to overcome "resh" and "Shin/sin"; it is TRUTH.

KNOW THE TRUTH AND THE TRUTH WILL SET YOU FREE

PSALM 119:164,165

Seven times a day do I praise thee because of thy righteous judgments. Great peace have they who love Thy law, and nothing shall offend them.

KJV

A WORD FROM ME: "Seven times a day" means "at all times". This means that at all times we should be in praise of the Holy One. He has decreed health and salvation to all who put their trust in Him; He has decreed Eternal Life through JESUS Christ, our LORD. Look around and re member the mighty works of GOD and be filled with praise. Morning, noon and night the whole world is filled with the creative wonders of the Hand of GOD. Why don't we see them? Because our eye is fixed on other things, rather than on the LORD. When we fix our eye on the LORD and His Word, then the whole of the beauty and power of GOD is revealed and we, in awesome wonder, praise Him.

Do you want to know the peace of GOD that passes all

understanding? Do you want to experience a life that is without offense or being offended? Then put your trust in the LORD GOD and feast on the riches of His Word; nothing will offend you and His Word will only offend those who are being convicted by the Holy Spirit unto salvation.

"Great peace" is that deep peace of the Spirit that is only known by those who have put their trust in the LORD and rest in His Word. When trouble blind-sides the devoted ones, they speak the Word of the LORD and nothing off-ends them. You notice that I used the divided word "offended" well when we are not stable we tend to be put off our feet; we are "off-ended". A divided heart will easily be off ended; this is why our heart must be fixed and stable in the LORD and His Word. How did JESUS address satan in the wilderness? He spoke the Word of the LORD. Nothing offended Him; He was fixed on the Word of His Father. We, too, have that tool and authority; we only have to use it. The Scripture says. "Thy word have I hidden in my heart, that I might not sin against Thee." When we read and study the Scripture, the Word takes root in our heart, so that in the fullness of time, the Holy Spirit can call it forth to bear fruit in our life.

STAND FIRM IN THE WORD OF TRUTH, BE STRONG AND ENDLESSLY PRAISE THE LORD.

PSALM 120:6, 7

My soul hath long dwelt with him that hateth peace. I am for peace; but when I speak, they are for war.

KJV

A WORD FROM ME: This is Ash Wednesday when I am writing this devotional. This is also the beginning of the "Songs of the Ascents" and the beginning of our "ascents" to Easter. How we ascend toward that Holy Day of Resurrection will change our life. So, let us begin where we are, in today's world; "I am for peace; but when I speak, they are for war."

    We dwell in a world that dwells in war and hates peace. The big struggle for humankind is to speak peace and pursue it, not to degrade to war. Our Spirit want peace and harmony and good will, but we are surrounded by those who say that the only way to peace is through war. This is false thinking and false living; it is contrary to everything that JESUS said and did and contrary to the whole of Biblical wisdom. Psalm 119 is an alphabetical path to life in GOD; Psalms 120-134 show us how to walk the path of GODLY living — "Ascents". This takes devotion and conviction to walk the path of peace in the land that wants war.

Commentaries says that, scriptural wisdom and deeds of kindness constitute the very basis of the world order, the alphabet of universal design. The individual who follows this comprehensive program will surely be elevated and will experience blessings and success, as Solomon said, 'The path of life for the wise leads upward (Proverbs 15:24)". I suggest that you read all of Proverbs 15:24, it is strong.

The LORD would have me follow this course and so I share it with you. This is not just a Lent discipline; it is a lifetime walk with the LORD, I call it, intentional living I will be teaching this for the Month of March and I know that I will gain insight, as I prepare this theme. It is radical and disciplined; I invite you to join me.

May your Lent be Holy, dedicated to "intentional living in the LORD".

YOUR THOUGHTS:

PSALM 121:3, 4

He will not allow your foot to slip; your Protector will not slumber. Behold, the Protector of Israel will neither slumber nor sleep.

BSB

A WORD FROM ME: I love to look into the original meaning of the Psalms from the Hebrew, because I find things that are often missed by other commentators; this is one of them. Psalm 121 is "a Psalm to the Ascents it is a Psalm of encouragement to those who 'make the Ascents to the World to Come'This it is encouragement to persevere in righteous living. Midrash Shocher Tov says, "This Psalm alludes to Israel's ultimate victory in the time of the Messiah, as foretold in Obadiah 1:21."

On a personal note, I love the word in the Hebrew text, Protector or "Guardian" The LORD GOD is our Guardian, as well as our friend and spouse. He guards us, by His Most Holy Spirit, day and night. He watches as we slumber and sleep, but

He never slumbers nor sleeps. While He watches, He guards us from all harm and stands in us as a standard against the onslaught of the enemy. He is our own, individual, Guardian; He is also the Guardian of our Nation and of the world. Therefore, we will not fear the terrors of night nor the pestilence that wastes in the noon day.

I had a real experience with the work of the Guardian. When I broke my wrist, I had surgery and developed an allergy to the anesthesia which caused mental anguish. One of the manifestations of that anguish was "night terrors" In the middle of one of those terrors, the LORD spoke to me, saying, "Fear not; I AM the Light in the darkness, I neither slumber nor sleep, I AM with you always." After that, I did not fear the night and slept soundly. You see, JESUS is the "I AM" Who is the Light that never slumbers or sleeps, but stands as your Guardian.

He is the Messiah Who gives us victory, through our LORD JESUS Christ.

Let this Psalm 121 be an encouragement to you, as you grow in grace and the love and knowledge of JESUS.

PSALM 122:1, 6-9

I was glad when they said unto me, "Let us go into the house of the LORD"... Pray for the peace of Jerusalem; they shall prosper who love thee. Peace be within thy walls, and prosperity within thy palaces. For my brethren and companions' sakes, I will now say "Peace be within thee. Because of the house of the LORD our GOD;
I will seek thy good.

KJV

A WORD FROM ME: Every Sunday morning, I arise at 5:30am to get to Church by 7:30am; why do I do that? Because I want to go and worship in the House of the LORD, with the LORD's people, I would move mountains to get there. This is the same passion that David exhibits in Psalm 122 and is a reflection of the passion of the Jewish people who said, "Let us go into the house of the LORD".

All my life, this passion to go into the House of the LORD has been part of my rhythm. It is a movement in my spirit that yearns to worship with others who are focused on the LORD. Corporate worship is a vital part of the life of Christians and was a vital part of the life of the Jewish People.

I have, in my lifetime, found depth to this passion; daily worship and daily intercession. Notice that David speaks of intercession in verses 6-9, where he says, "PRAY FOR ..." Worship of the LORD GOD and intercession for others, go hand in hand. This should be a part of our daily rhythm of life, WORSHIP AND INTERCESSION.

There is another meaning that I have found to the rhythm of worship and intercession; not just daily, but "without ceasing". The secret lies in Whom we worship and in Whom we "live and move and have our being". Do we recognize that JESUS is always present, every moment of every day, all the time? Then we are in the Presence of the Holy One, so our Worship is without ceasing, everywhere and at all time. What is the quality of our Worship? Is it casual and surface, only acknowledging Him when we need Him? Or is it true Worship and intercession, coming from a heart fixed on the LORD?

I am helping my husband do income tax, am I doing this task (which is difficult for me) as unto the LORD as part of my worship of Him? If I am in the heart of Worship, then this task is anointed by the LORD and He "will direct my path".

When I worked as the Executive Director of Yavapai Center for the Blind in Prescott, the LORD showed me that the paperwork tasks, that I had to perform, were really people or about people and should be handled with prayer. Even a request for funding from the State, had to do with people and meeting their needs; this was GOD business. Every task that we perform is an act of Worship and intercession. This is the high road of life and the righteous walk there (Isaiah 35:8) Brethren and companions, let us walk there.

Pray for peace, pray for inner peace, and pray for your brethren and companions; "Worship the LORD in the beauty of Holiness, let the whole earth stand in awe of Him"

PSALM 123:1-4

Unto Thee lift up mine eyes, O Thou who dwellest in the heavens. Behold, as the eye of servants look unto the hand of their masters, and as the eyes of a maiden unto the hand of her mistress, so our eyes wait upon the LORD our GOD, until He has mercy upon us. Have mercy upon us, O LORD, have mercy upon us; for we are exceedingly filled with contempt. Our soul is exceedingly filled with the scoffing of those who are at ease, and with the contempt of the proud.

KJV

A WORD FROM ME: Today, I ponder the words: "servant" and "friends" (John 15: 13-17) This Psalm calls me to be a faithful "servant" who does not take the eye off the hand of the master/mistress; is always watching for the LORD GOD to move, so we can follow. This is the truth and we, like JESUS are to be watchful for the movement of the LORD GOD and follow His Word, His lead and His ways.

JESUS said, Ye are My friends, if you do whatever I command you. Henceforth I call you not servants; for the servant knoweth not what his lord doeth; but have called you friends; for all things that I have heard of My Father I have made known unto you. Ye have not chosen Me, but I have chosen you, and ordained you, that ye should go and bring forth fruit, and that your fruit should remain; that whatever ye shall ask of the Father in My Name, He may give it you. These things I command you, that ye love one another.

Servants have their eye on the Master and friends are those who are very close to the Master and know His Heart. JESUS was both servant and friend of humankind and I believe that we are to be both to all people and to GOD.

JESUS always took the road of humility (servant) and He shared His Heart with all who would listen to Him (friendship). I see the washing of feet of all people as a servant act and bringing the Gospel to all, as being the highest form of friendship.

When we are faced with contempt on the part of others or find that that spirit arising in us, we must look to the Master and find in Him the LOVE to embrace the other with unconditional love. This is the ac of the servant, who desires that all come to the love that is in Christ JESUS and be saved.

There is a statement that I hold dear: Preach the Gospel, and sometimes use words.

PSALM 124:6-8

Blessed be the LORD, Who hath not given us as a prey to their teeth. Our soul is escaped like bird out of the snare of the fowlers; the snare is broken, and we are escaped. Our help is in the Name of the LORD, who made heaven and earth.

KJV

A WORD FROM ME: This is a true story and one of you, reading this, will recognize it. I have a dear friend who was in a bad marriage relation ship. She was afraid and terrified almost every day. One day, she saw a bird in a cage and it was clear, as she recounted it to me, that she was that bird. Suddenly, the door flew open and the bird flew away, the snare was broken and she would escape. Yes, she did escape and is living free now; highly blessed by GOD.

Blessed be the LORD, Who has not given us as a prey to the teeth of the wicked. The LORD GOD, Blessed be He, has prepared a way of escape to those who call upon His Name. The LORD is the Creator of heaven and earth; all power is His and we are His Children. He opens the doors of the prison cells in which we find ourselves; there is no prison that can keep in bondage those who call upon His Name.

If you are going through a difficult time in your life, call upon JESUS and He will open the way for you to fly above the storm and be safe in the shelter of His Hand. I have been meditating on the verse from Isaiah 49: 16: I have engraved thee upon the palms of My hands; thy walls are continually before Me. Not just one palm of His Hand, but the palms of His Hands. Everywhere He goes and everything He does, we are there, engraved upon His palms. Whenever He looks at His Hands, He sees us; whenever He touches with His power, we are there. Why don't we feel like it? Why do we feel out of touch with the mighty works of GOD? Because we are not united to Him in the present moment.

GOD is here in every moment of our life, He carries us on the palms of His Hands, but are we looking elsewhere? Are we looking at our past, with its hurts and misses or are we looking at the future, hoping for a manifestation of the LORD? What about looking at the present and seeing JESUS walking in the cool of the evening in our heart? What about sitting with Him in the Garden and listening to Him talk? What about yielding our self to His direction and letting Him see through our eyes and touch through our hands NOW, in the present moment? Then you will see the manifestation of the Creator of Heaven and Earth move in miracles TODAY.

PSALM 125:1, 2

They who trust in the LORD shall be as Mount Zion, which cannot be removed, but abideth forever. As the mountains are round about Jerusalem, so the LORD is round about His people from henceforth even forever.

A WORD FROM ME: When I look at the mountains every morning, from my window, I see the everlasting hills, that saw the history of this area and was there when antelope played on the plains and Indians built their pueblos. The mountains heard the cry of the newborn and the mourning cry of the passing of a beloved member of the tribe. The mountains stretch out and surround the town, with their strength.

The Psalmist looked at the mountains of Zion and saw them as the Hand of GOD, protecting the people. It was a sign of strength and longevity or all those who saw the mighty mountains. GOD, who created the mountains, is stronger and more powerful; He speaks and mountains become dust or dust becomes mountains. When we look at the mountains, we should look first at the One who created them and give praise to Him who is above the mountains.

As I am writing this, I see a mountain called "the skull" upon which the King of Glory was crucified. His Blood ran down to the ground and bathed it in new creation. Yes, JESUS redeemed the ground by His Blood and the stones cried out, "PRAISE THE LORD". The rocks split as they cried out in Glory to GOD; what man had made with his hands was rent in two from top to bottom and the Holy of Holies was made manifest to all.

When you look at the mountains, see the LORD of Hosts, the King of Glory, riding on His white Stallion with the hosts of heaven, and see Him bring all things into right order. This is our GOD, Who surrounds and protects His own with more strength than the everlasting hills. Praise ye the LORD with all creation; Laud and magnify Him, bow before Him Who is worthy of all praise. PRAISE YE THE LORD!

Your Thoughts:

PSALM 126

When the LORD turned again the captivity of Zion, we were like them that dream. Then was our mouth filled with laughter and our tongue with singing; then said they among the nations, "The LORD hath done great things for them". The LORD hath done great things for us, whereof we are glad. Turn again our captivity, O LORD, like the streams of the Negev. THEY THAT SOW IN TEARS SHALL REAP IN JOY. He that goeth forth and weepeth, bearing precious seed, shall doubtless come again with rejoicing bringing His sheaves with him.

KJV

A WORD FROM ME: There is an old song that we sing at thanksgiving time: "Bringing in the sheaves, we shall come rejoicing, bringing in the sheaves." Yes, you have to plant seed in order to have a harvest, and sometimes, the planting of that seed is with weeping. The ground is hard, due to being fallow through the resting time, so it needs to be tilled before it is sown and that is hard work. Tilling is back-breaking work, digging in dirt and pulling out the weeds, rocks and clods. In order to have a good harvest, the precious seed must be sown in good ground, which receives the seed with gladness. A happy ground is a fertile ground.

So it is with the heart; if the heart is hard, and set on its own wishes, wants and desires, then the precious seed will fall on hard ground and will not bear much fruit. If the heart is soft and willing to be made fertile by the hand of the plowman and good mulch, then the harvest will be plenteous. I have heard a saying that, "It takes a lot of fertilizer to grow an Oak tree" Adversity is the fertilizer in the heart of the one who loves the LORD.

Yes, the LORD uses adversity and false accusations to soften the ground of our heart. The accuser of the Brethren stands before the LORD of Hosts, accusing the brethren day and night, but the LORD uses false accusations to soften the soil of the heart, so that it can receive the precious seed of new life. There are things that have to die before the resurrection; there are old clods that have to be broken up, before the seed can find good ground. "Except a grain of wheat fall into the ground and die, it abideth alone; but if it dies, it bringeth forth much fruit," There are things in the heart that must die before the good fruit is formed and revealed. There are relationships that must die, before there can be a resurrection and new life. The weeping time is the dying time; the rejoicing time is the harvest, BUT WE MUST WAIT PATIENT LY FOR THE TIME TO GATHER IN THE HARVEST. WE WAIT UPON THE LORD, GLORIOUS DAY OF RESURRECTION!!!

PSALM 127

Unless the Lord builds the house, They labor in vain who build it; Unless the Lord guards the city, The watchman stays awake in vain. It is vain for you to rise up early, To sit up late, To eat the bread of sorrows; For so He gives His beloved sleep. Behold, children are a heritage from the Lord, The fruit of the womb is a reward. Like arrows in the hand of a warrior, So are the children of one's youth. Happy is the man who has his quiver full of them; They shall not be ashamed, But shall speak with their enemies in the gate.

NKJV

A WORD FROM ME: Please hear these words deep in your heart.

First, man must realize that all human effort is futile if it is not blessed with Divine approval and assistance...

Troubles come in all families, but the LORD knows the deep

and secret reasons and meaning behind the trouble; He will work it out when all faith and factors are placed in His Hand. For us to try to figure it out is vain imaginations and a useless waste of time; time is a gift from GOD. The quicker that all things are put in the Hand of JESUS, the faster that His love will prevail. You see, His Divine Love is the key to all efforts, He desires success for every one of His Children. As a Good and Loving Father, He will create the perfect balance in all situations; trust Him to make all things work together for good, for those who love Him and magnify His Holy Name.

Life is not in our hand, that we could manipulate it through our own power and control. Life is in the Hand of GOD who gives us life and breath. Every aspect of our living, which is given under the control of GOD, will be blessed by Him and adorned with His goodness, beauty and glory. Trust JESUS in this, trust Him with y our life, He is worthy of all our trust. He will build the house, provide a good living and raise good children through His wisdom imparted to those who trust Him.

PSALM 128:1, 2

Blessed is every one that feareth the LORD that walketh in His ways. For thou shalt eat the labor of thine hands; happy shalt thou be, and it shall be well with thee.

KJV

A WORD FROM ME: I just activated the prayer team for the people of Boston in the wake of the tragedy at the Boston Marathon; then I read these words from Psalm 128. What can I write in the wake of this horror? What words can give strength to those who are hurting, right now? Then I stopped and looked at the words from this Psalm: "Blessed is everyone that feareth the LORD that walketh in His ways." The Scripture calls us from looking at the "storm" to looking deeply into the face of JESUS. These words call us to a deeper level of living; "walking in His ways". I cried for those who were harmed: I mourned for those runners who lost limbs and might never run again. I was a runner and know how valuable arms and legs are and how much time goes into developing those limbs for a marathon; BUT GOD is calling us to look deeply into the Face of JESUS and walk with Him in intercession for others with His Love.

Yes, we are called to love with His Love, unconditionally; we are called to show mercy with His mercy, unconditionally; we are called to give grace with His grace, unconditionally; we are called to pray for those in Boston as though we were in the body with them.

"For I am persuaded that neither death, nor life, nor angels, nor principalities, nor powers, nor things present, nor things to come, nor height, nor depth, nor any other creation, shall be able to separate us from the love of GOD, which is in Christ JESUS, our LORD." (Romans 8: 38, 39)

Let us go forth as witnesses of that unconditional love of JESUS, and pray with His Love for others. The "fear of the LORD" is humble adoration of the Holy One; let us humble ourselves in the sight of the LORD, bringing with us those who suffer, and He has promised to raise us and them up; this is Resurrection Power found only in JESUS, who was raised from the dead and made the way for us to live with Him.

May the resurrection power of the Holy Spirit be with us and the people of Boston, New York, Atlanta, Pennsylvania and all parts of the world, who are living in fear and terror; LORD have mercy, Christ have mercy; LORD have mercy. "There is no fear in love, but perfect love casts out fear for fear has torment." LET US LOVE ONE ANOTHER.

PSALM 129:4

The LORD is righteous; He hath cut asunder the cords of the wicked.

KJV

A WORD FROM ME: I want to begin this week with a parable from ancient Jewish literature:

> A farmer once lent his ox to a neighbor, but the neighbor took advantage of the favor and over worked the ox. He permitted his ten sons to plow with the ox in succession without allowing the exhausted animal to rest. Finally, the ox collapsed under the yoke. When the owner came to claim his ox, and saw it crushed beneath its burden, he didn't pause to berate his irresponsible neighbor; his first thought was for the animal's welfare. He ran over and smashed the yoke and cut the harness ropes.

I told this parable to illustrate the Heart of GOD, Who thinks first about His children and cuts the "cords" that bind. Notice the fact that the ox had collapsed and it was only the work of the farmer that freed the ox; thus it is with us, only the work of GOD can free us from the bondage of wickedness. He, alone, cuts the binding cords; He, alone, sees our plight and delivers us from every evil.

What can we do? We must yield to GOD and His power to deliver; let Him work His work, cutting cords and raising up the collapsed child of GOD. Like the ox in the parable, He will run to His Child before He addresses the abuse; but the abuser will be dealt with in time and it may surprise us as to how the abuser is dealt a judgment. Could it be that the abuser would be converted to JESUS and be saved, then show compassion rather than abuse? Could it be that the witness of compassion for the collapsed child (ox, in the parable) would soften the heart of the abuser and he would come to JESUS?

We must always look at JESUS as the one who loves unconditionally; His love never fails. Remember the words of JESUS on the cross: FATHER, FORGIVE THEM FOR THEY KNOW NOT WHAT THEY DO.

PSALM 130

If out of the depths have I called to You, O LORD; LORD, hear my voice; let your ears consider well the voice of my supplication. You, LORD, were to note what is done amiss, O LORD, who could stand?

For there is forgiveness with You; therefore You shall be feared.

I wait for the LORD; my soul waits for Him; in His Word is my hope. My soul waits for the LORD, more than watchmen for the morning, more than watchmen for the morning. O Israel, wait for the LORD, for with the LORD there is mercy; with Him there is plenteous redemption, and He shall redeem Israel from all their sins.

DE PROFUNDIS - OUT OF THE DEPTH

A WORD FROM ME: JESUS said, "A good man, out of the good treasure of his heart, bringeth forth that which is good; and an evil man, out of the evil treasure of his heart, bringeth forth that which is evil; for out of the abundance of the heart the mouth speaketh."(Luke 6:45)

I began this discussion on Psalm 130 with the words of JESUS about the heart, because I see in this Psalm two understandings of "De Profundis - out of the depth" as being the work of the heart.

We can look at the first verses of this Psalm as a cry for help or we can look at these verses as a call to Worship. We all have walked through the dark place of hurt and harm; we have all cried unto the LORD for help and deliverance. In our pain and broken heart we cry out to GOD, "LORD, hear our prayer and let our cry come unto You". Have we thought that this "broken heart" is what we should have when we Worship the LORD in the beauty of His Holiness? The broken heart is open and humble; it is not proud and exalted; it radiates "de profundis"; the words, "I'm only a sinner saved by grace." Some will say, "Are we to walk around with a gloomy look on our face, head bowed and hunched over in grief?" No, we are the redeemed of the LORD, Who has shown mercy to us and plenteous redemption, through JESUS Christ the LORD.

The Blood of JESUS has reconciled us to GOD; therefore, we have joy and gladness in our heart. However, our worship must be from the broken heart, wide open and humble before the LORD, Who has done it all for us. Joy must be from "de profundis" our words must be from "de profundis," and our actions must be from "de profundis"; anything else is pride and arrogance. The Grace of the LORD is not cheap, but it is free (Bonhoeffer) we are not to take our free gift as a call to self-exaltation. Note: Luke 18: 9-14 the parable of the Pharisee and publican.

DE PROFUNDIS - OUT OF THE DEPTH WE WORSHIP YOU, O LORD; LORD HEAR OUR CRY OF LOVE FOR YOU.

Your Thoughts:

PSALM 131

My heart is not proud, Lord, my eyes are not haughty; I do not concern myself with great matters or things too wonderful for me. But I have calmed and quieted myself, I am like a weaned child with its mother; like a weaned child I am content. Israel, put your hope in the Lord both now and forevermore.

NIV

A WORD FROM ME: The image of the helpless child, needing to rely on mother for everything in life, is a very good image for us to embrace in our relationship with the LORD GOD. The nursing child is totally helpless and entirely dependent upon his mother, so we are to be to tally dependent upon GOD. Even the weaned child, who has achieved independence from the mother, will stick close to her, needing for her to provide the daily provision. Thus it is with our relationship with GOD. We are to hope to GOD.

N the Hebrew, I was interested in this phrase "hope to HASHEM" and so I did some pondering about this; our usual phrase is "hope in the LORD," what is the difference? "To HASHEM" speaks to me of distance from GOD, the person speaking (David) feels distant from GOD, but like Him, nursing at GOD like an infant. "In GOD" speaks to me of intimate relationship; the nursing child feels like they are one with the mother and the mother one with the child. I feel that this oneness comes to us through the relationship established in JESUS Christ, who broke down the wall of separation by His Blood. We are one with GOD and GOD is one with us, therefore, we hope in GOD.

The nursing child accepts everything that comes from the mother and is filled with all he needs. The child is still and open, humble and silent. One of the worse times that I had as a nursing mother was when my child was fitful; grabbing and clawing, biting and gnawing. The child did not get good nourishment and I did not get peace from the relationship. It was awful! So it is with our relationship with GOD. When we grab and claw, bite and gnaw we do not get the peace and silence, openness and filling that comes with submission and yielding. Even the weaned child hovers by its mother, so we should be with GOD, no distance from Him, living IN Him, totally dependent on Him.

It is pride and self-exaltation that keeps us from the silence of the soul and the rest that comes from living in GOD. Humility acknowledges dependence and we must be humble before the LORD and before one another. Casting out pride and self-exaltation, and embracing openness and yielding, brings the temperament we need, in order to be filled full with everything that GOD has for us.

I would love to know what you think, then I could be edified by your wisdom.

PSALM 132:13-18

For the LORD hath chosen Zion; He hath desired it for His habitation. This is My rest forever; here will I dwell; for I have desired it. I will abundantly bless her provision; I will satisfy her poor with bread. I will also clothe her priests with salvation; and her saints shall shout aloud for joy. There will I make the horn of David to bud; I have ordained a lamp for Mine anointed. His enemies will I clothe with shame, but upon Himself shall His crown flourish.

KJV

A WORD FROM ME: The LORD GOD has said that He will do wonderful things for His Children. As an adopted Child of the Living GOD, by the Blood of the Only Begotten Son, JESUS, these promises are for the Christian (Ephesians 1 :3-14) These promises are yea and Amen; established by the Word of GOD.

GOD has chosen us and desired us for His place to live

(Know you not that you are the Temple of the Living GOD who is within you) by the Holy Spirit. GOD rests in us and lives there, by the Holy Spirit Who is within us. He will abundantly bless our provision and will satisfy the poor with enough provision to meet all the needs. Those who testify of Him, teach and preach the Gospel, will be clothed in His salvation and all those who believe in Him will shout for joy. He has provided salvation through JESUS Christ the LORD, who came through the line of David. JESUS is the Light and the Lamp stand for the light; we are illumined by Him to be a light in the world.

Those who reject JESUS will be put to shame; those who believe in the LORD JESUS will flourish, for His Crown will flourish. Everything good in life is found in JESUS; He is the Way, the Truth and the Life; no man cometh unto the Father except through Him. We walk in the Light, because JESUS is the Light; we walk in truth, because JESUS is the Truth and we live, because JESUS is Life eternal.

Sunday is Pentecost Sunday, when we remember the coming of the Holy Spirit, sent from GOD. I pray that you will receive a mighty anointing of the Holy Spirit upon you and your family. May the LORD grant you His grace.

PSALM 133

Behold, how good and how pleasant it is for brethren to dwell together in unity! It is like the precious ointment upon the head, that ran down upon the beard, even Aarons beard; that went down to the skirts of his garments, like the dew of Hermon, and like the dew that descended upon the mountains of Zion; for there the LORD commanded the blessing, even life forevermore.

KJV

A WORD FROM ME: "How good and how pleasant it is for brethren to dwell together in unity!" Unity in what? Isn't it better to say, unity in Whom? There are many who say that unity means compromise; you give up your place and I give up mine and we will be in unity together, if we embrace the middle ground. I say that there is a much better way; Unity in the

LORD JESUS Christ, by His Holy Spirit. GOD has no middle ground; it is His way or no way at all.

What happens when we are in unity in JESUS? What is the result of being in one accord, in one place in JESUS? Read Acts 2: 1-4. The followers of JESUS, (that is who we are) were in one accord and in one place and the Holy Spirit came in power to anoint each one of them. Yes, that is the meaning of the verses that follow in Psalm 133; unity in the Holy Spirit is like precious ointment (oil) that runs down from our head to our toes with the anointing of GOD upon us. Anointed to do what? To preach the Gospel of JESUS Christ and to carry His witness into the world.

This is a Psalm of Pentecost. The Holy Spirit is anointing those who dwell in unity in the LORD JESUS Christ. He is anointing us with gifts and with fruit to offer to the hurting and starving world. This is empowerment to go forth and to be His witness; go forth in the Name and anointing of the Holy Spirit.

We are the bearers of the water of life to others who are thirsty and wilting from the scorching heat of life. We must, however, stay in unity in the Holy Spirit of GOD and His Holy Scripture. Departure from the Household of Faith in JESUS means that we no longer carry the water of life and the anointing of GOD.

The LORD Bless you and keep you, the LORD make His face to shine upon you and give you His peace; both now and forever more.

PSALM 134

Behold, bless ye the LORD, all ye servants of the LORD, who by night stand in the house of the LORD. Lift up your hands in the sanctuary, and bless the LORD. The LORD, Who made heaven and earth, bless thee out of Zion.

KJV

"The genuine servant of HASHEM is completely reliable and never abandons his post. Not only does he act as a guardian of the faith by day, in the times of ease and success, but even at night, in times of adversity and gloom, he remains a guard and refuses to fall asleep."

MALBIM

A WORD FROM ME: Devotion is an uncommon word for today. We seem to move along and even speak at such a fast pace that it is hard to be still, faithful and stand, unless we are compelled to do so. Devotion to GOD should compel us.

Malbim captures something that is very important about the "servant of the LORD"; "not only does he act as a guardian of the faith by day, in times of ease and success, but even at night, in times of adversity and gloom." The devout person is not a "fair weather friend" of GOD. The devout person is so thankful to GOD for His great goodness, that he never stops praising GOD, day or night — good times or bad.

A woman I know was very sick, her family wanted to put her in the hospital, but she had to prepare a commentary for her dear friends. So she prayed and the LORD gave her favor to write the commentary and then take care of her sickness. She was healed as she remembered the LORD Who made heaven and earth — bless His Holy Name.

As servants of the LORD, we are to wait upon Him with the devotion of a thankful person. He has provided everything that we need in life and He has asked only one thing in return; our love. He has given us so much, that our love for Him should be reflected in devout living of joy and celebration; lifting up holy hands in the presence of the LORD.

PSALM 135:1, 2

Praise the LORD. Praise the name of the LORD; praise him, you servants of the LORD, you who minister in the house of the LORD, in the courts of the house of our God.

NIV

THINK ABOUT IT: The name of the Lord is Holy. So Holy that the devout do not casually speak his name.

One of the commandments states that we are not to take His name in vain. The Third Commandment stated by the Lord is: "Thou shalt not take the name of the LORD thy God in vain; for the LORD will not hold him guiltless that taketh his name in vain."

So many people do not honor the Holiness of the name of the Lord using it without care, thought or honor.

As I meditated on this thought about respecting the Name

of the Lord, I realized that disrespecting His name is an indicator of the relationship a person has with Him.

If you love someone, you speak kindly about them; However, if you don't care about them, you speak casually, or do not speak about them at all. The degree of meaning a person holds in their heart, is reflected in their speech.

Remember when you were first in love with another, you glowed with joy, just hearing their name. Do you glow with joy at the Name of Jesus? Is His Name sweet to you? Do you adore Him?

Think about it!!

PSALM 136:1, 2

O give thanks unto the LORD, for He is good; for His mercy endureth forever. Oh, give thanks unto the GOD of gods; for His mercy endureth forever.

KJV

A WORD FROM ME: The Hebrew renders the word "mercy" as "kindness". I want to look at the kindness of GOD toward us. In His kindness, the LORD GOD created all things; in His kindness, He sustained all things; in His kindness, He redeemed all things; in His kindness, He delivers all things FOREVER AND FOREVER. GOD provided and still provides everything that is needed for life and for our salvation; there is not a thing that He withholds from those who love Him. His presence is always with us and forever will be, because of His kindness. The Holy One, who is above all, loves with a love that is without limits, He is faithful and passionate about us. He is so passionate, that He gave His highest and His best, His only begotten Son, for the redemption of the world. He bought us back from the jaws of death by the Blood of His own Son. The Mercy Seat of GOD is covered with the Blood of His Son, so that all who believe in JESUS are saved from wrath.

Oh, my dear sisters and brothers in Christ, what can we do to give enough thanks for all that the LORD GOD has given us? We can give Him our life as a token of our thanks. "But what I can I give Him, give my heart."

Oh, give thanks to the LORD, for He is good; for His mercy endureth forever. AMEN.

PSALM 137:4

How shall we sing the LORD'S song in a foreign land?

NIV

A WORD FROM ME: "HOW?" we sing with our heart. Singing and making melody; dancing and praising the LORD does not have to be physical. As a matter of fact, all physical expression must come from the heart, in order to be acceptable, heard, and seen by the LORD.

The only foreign land is the land of darkness, inhabited by the devil and his angels. So............... what are you doing in that foreign land? Sing and make melody unto the LORD JESUS in your heart and the darkness will vanish. Sing about the Blood of JESUS; sing about the glory of the LORD; sing about the endless wonders of our GOD; sing in the heart. Glorify GOD with every fiber of our being, be the Light that defeats the darkness of this world - Sing, sisters and brother; dance in the heart, sisters and brothers. Light up the world with the Glory of GOD.

"How shall we sing the LORD'S song in a foreign land?" With the loud voice of praise and thanksgiving in a grateful heart unto the LORD, sing it loud and clear; don't hold back. There is no "foreign land" in the heart that dwells in the land of the LORD GOD; so dwell in His Sanctuary, live in His presence and SING.

I have been having fun using sign language instead of my voice. I have learned a few signs and I use them often: JESUS is LORD, the LORD GOD almighty, and thank you JESUS, are the signs I know best. I can sing them all day long.

How shall we sing the songs of the LORD? FROM THE HEART!!!!!!

PSALM 138:2, 8

I will worship toward Thy holy temple, and praise Thy Name for Thy loving-kindness and for Thy truth; for Thou hast magnified Thy Word above all Thy Name... The LORD will perfect that which concerneth me. Thy mercy, O LORD, endureth forever; forsake not the works of thine own hands.

KJV

A WORD FROM ME: Do you trust GOD with your life? Do you trust GOD in everything? If so, then the worship of Him and Who He is, is as natural as breathing. The LORD GOD is truth, He cannot lie; the LORD GOD is faithful, He cannot back down from what He says; the LORD GOD is trustworthy, He will do what He says and He says that He loves you and desires the best for you. "He has magnified His word above all His name."

I have been pondering the words, "Magnify His Word above all His Name." and I have found a key to worship and obedience. If GOD, Almighty, honors His Word above Himself, then, I can rely on the fact that when GOD speaks, He will accomplish that which He has said. If He says, "By the stripes of JESUS you are healed" then you are healed; if He says that He will put all your enemies under your feet, then He will do it; If He says, "Fear not" then why do you tremble in fear? Believe GOD, He stands by His Word. He magnifies His word above all his Name.

What does it mean when it says, "The LORD will perfect that which concerneth me?" I believe that GOD has a plan for each of us; a plan to prosper us and not to harm us, to give us peace and an expected end. (Jeremiah 29:11) His plan is perfect and He has thought it through to the minutest portion. Anything that does not conform to His plan must be amended, by us or Him. I believe that yielding to Him, as JESUS did, "Nevertheless not my will but Thy will be done," is the human part of conforming to the plan of GOD.

There is another thought about "The LORD will perfect that which concerneth me"; He, by the Holy Spirit, will take our prayers and petitions and make them perfect before the Father; yes, even our prayers are made perfect by GOD.

The LORD GOD will never forsake the work of His hand. His love and grace; tender-mercy and kindness will always surround those who put their trust in Him. TRUST AND OBEY, FOR THERE'S NO OTHER WAY TO BE HAPPY IN JESUS; BUT TO TRUST AND OBEY.

PSALM 139:17, 18

How precious also are Thy thoughts unto me, O GOD! How great is the sum of them! If I should count them, they are more in number than the sand; when I awake, I am still with Thee.

KJV

A WORD FROM ME: The LORD GOD thinks "precious thoughts" about us. These are not just "precious moments" these are timeless, and end less thoughts about us. The LORD GOD has plans for our good and a vision of a joy-filled life. All the blessings and benefits of GOD, found in the Holy Scripture, are for us, today; all we have to do is receive them.

"When I awake" can have different meanings; it can mean that when I have slept through the night, the LORD is still there when I awake from slumber. It can also mean that when I awake to the fact that the LORD loves me, totally, that the

LORD is right there, just like He has always been. Both understandings have merit and are true.

There is a certain comfort in knowing that we can fall asleep in the arms of GOD and when we awaken we are in His presence, He never leaves us nor forsakes us. It is also comforting to know that I do not have to know everything pertaining to GOD; all I need to do is trust Him to give me what I need when I need it. Jeremiah 33:3 says, "Call upon Me, and I will answer thee, and show thee great and mighty things, which thou knowest not." Imaginations and speculations about things and people are worthless use of the time GOD has given us; to speak of them is worthless use of the breath He has provided. He will enlighten all of us through His Word with a Word fit for the opportunity. Trust Him to be right there all of the time, instructing us by His truth.

The LORD GOD thinks precious thoughts about us; Jeremiah 29: 11 says, "I know the thoughts that I think toward you, saith the LORD, thoughts of peace, and not evil, to give you an expected end." That "expected end" is Eternal life with JESUS. JESUS purchased our eternal life by His precious Blood. He loved us so much that He willingly laid down his life for us; bridging the gap between GOD and man.

Only receive Him in total surrender to His will and feel the peace of knowing that GOD has all things in His control. GOD has a control issue; He is in control of all things for the good of all.

PSALM 140:1-3, 12-13

Deliver me, O LORD, from the evil man, and preserve me from the violent man, who imagine mischiefs in their heart; continually, are they gathered together for war. They have sharpened their tongues like a serpent; adders poison is under their lips.
(12, 13) I know that the LORD will maintain the cause of the afflicted, and the right of the poor. Surely, the righteous shall give thanks unto Thy Name; the upright shall dwell in Thy presence.

KJV

A WORD FROM ME: As I was looking at other translations of these verses, I discovered that there are two meanings to the first two verses. One would have us understand that "evil man" mean all people who plot evil; the other understanding is that there is one evil entity that causes violence and mischief, poisoning the hearts of people.

I prefer the second understanding. Evil is perpetrated by the evil one, the devil. JESUS was very clear about that. Therefore, those who do evil are victims of an evil presence; yes, they are willing victims. Evil, darkness, violence, war, hate, hurt, harm and all forms of destruction are the work of one source, Satan. How do we defeat Satan and end his work?

Satan was defeated on the Cross by the Son of GOD shedding His Blood for the remission of sin. When JESUS said, "It is finished" that was the end of Satan. How do we defeat Satan? By living in the presence of JESUS and pleading His Blood over us and over all who oppose Him. Yes, those who oppose us, oppose JESUS. JESUS said, "Whatsoever you do to the least of my brothers, that you do unto Me."

The poison of the serpent tongue is neutralized by the antidote of the Blood of the Holy Son of GOD. No weapon that is formed against those who put their trust in JESUS, will ever prevail. We are above and not beneath; we are victors not victims; JESUS is our sure defense. We have the authority to command Satan to "be gone" in the Name of JESUS. We, also, have the authority to pray for those who are being used by the enemy to hurt, and harm others.

When you understand that wicked people are victims of the evil one, it is easier to forgive them for they know not what they do. If they knew what they were doing, they would not yield themselves to the control of the enemy. "Father, forgive them for they know not what they do." Walk in love and forgiveness; light and truth; giving thanks to the Lord for He is goodness and mercy.

YOUR THOUGHTS:

PSALM 141:1-3

LORD, I cry unto Thee; make haste unto me; give ear unto my voice, when I cry unto Thee. Let my prayer be set forth before Thee as incense; and the lifting up of my hands, as the evening sacrifice.
Set a watch, O LORD, before my mouth; keep the door of my lips.

KJV

A WORD FROM ME: As I am reading this Psalm, I am hearing the words of Jeremiah 33:3, "Call unto me, and I will answer thee, and show thee great and mighty things, which thou knowest not". Do you believe that? When you call unto the LORD He answers you and shows you great and mighty things, which thou knowest not; do you believe that? I do!!!!!!

Let me tell you a personal testimony; this just happened to me this week. I was crying unto the LORD for help and wisdom in a troubling matter; then I waited for an answer. I remembered a verse in Genesis which caused me to examine my thoughts and attitude. Look at Genesis 3: 9-11 and notice the two questions asked by GOD to Adam; "Where art Thou?" and "Who told you that thou wast naked?" The first question called me to look at the attitude and thoughts of my heart; they were stinking, so I repented of these vain imaginations and the waste of GOD's time that I had caused. I repented with tears and great sorrow. The second question caused me to tremble; "Who told you this?" Well, the LORD could not have told me all the stinking stuff that I was thinking, so it must have come from an evil source. When I looked at all the time that I had spent in ruminating on the evil thoughts, I was sick.

The lesson in this story is that we must "Guard our Heart" from vain imaginations and those things that are not Scriptural. The LORD has given us His Holy Word, so that we have a source to check our heart-life and our thoughts. When a thought or a deeds tempt us to go against the Word of the LORD, cast them out and do not entertain them even for a moment. Little evil thoughts can become grownup sins quickly, so kick them out.

When you experience depression of any kind, say, "Where art thou, O heart and mind?" And then say, "Who told you that?" To end depression, say, to the first question, "I dwell in the secret place of the Most High," "I praise Thee O GOD and worship Thee; I exalt your Holy Name; blessed be the Name of the LORD." And to the second question say, "The Holy Scripture of the LORD, His Holy Word, says so; I believe that the LORD said so; I believe, help Thou mine unbelief." In my case the depression vanished and Light shone in my heart. I lifted up my hands as an evening sacrifice. The LORD has kept the door of my lips, so that I praise Him continually.

PSALM 142:1, 2

I cried unto the LORD with my voice; with my voice unto the LORD did I make my supplication. I poured out my complaint before Him; I showed before Him my trouble.

A WORD FROM ME: It is a sign of total trust in the LORD to "cry unto the LORD with my voice." Notice that the Psalmist did not cry unto men for help in his time of need; He cried unto the LORD. When we "pour out our complaint before the Lord," we are saying that we trust Him to answer and to help in the situation. "In Thee, O LORD, do I put my trust; let me never be confounded" is the cry of the believer.

Let's look at the "believer"; the believer in JESUS Christ, trusts that the LORD will provide. The "believer" does not doubt that the LORD knows what is right and best. The "believer" knows that the LORD will defend and protect His Children against any source of hurt or harm. The "believer" stands on the promises of GOD.

Do you notice that the Psalmist does not try to influence the result of the prayer? He does not say, "LORD, I want you to do it this way." In stead, the whole Psalm is an affirmation of the grandeur of the LORD, His way is righteous and Holy. It is only at the end, that the Psalmist asks that the LORD bring His soul out of prison. A freed soul can praise the LORD with abundance and that is the desire of the heart of the Psalmist.

I am struck by the "desire of the heart" Is it your desire of your heart to praise the LORD in the land of the Living? Is it your desire of your heart to show forth the love of GOD to all people? Is it your desire of your heart to serve the LORD in the beauty of Holiness? You see, what is in the heart is what is seen of GOD. What is GOD seeing? What is your heart's desire?

Mine is to serve and please the LORD and to live according to His Word, so that all who see will believe that He is and loves them as He loves me.

PSALM 143:9-12

Rescue me from my enemies, LORD, for I hide myself in you. Teach me to do your will, for you are my God; may your good Spirit lead me on level ground. For your name's sake, LORD, preserve my life; in your righteousness, bring me out of trouble. In your unfailing love, silence my enemies; destroy all my foes, for I am your servant.

NIV

THINK ABOUT IT: David reminds us that the Lord God is our hiding place, where we can be sheltered from harm. The Lord God is our teacher so that we can learn the way and will of God. David understands that the Holy Spirit will lead him into all truth and set his feet on "level ground."

David also understands that he is alive and put in the place of leadership for the sake of the Name of the Lord. He says, "Preserve my life for your name sake."

David lived his life as an instrument of the Lord. He was dependent on the Lord and his security rested in the righteousness and faithfulness of God. This is why David is known as a "Man after Gods own heart."

Do we live our life for His Holy name's sake? If so, what does that look like?

Write about it and live it for His name's sake.

Your Thoughts

PSALM 144:1,-4

Praise be to the LORD my Rock, who trains my hands for war, my fingers for battle. He is my loving God and my fortress, my stronghold and my deliverer, my shield, in whom I take refuge, who subdues peoples under me. Lord, what are human beings that you care for them, They are like a breath; their days are like a fleeting shadow.

NIV

THINK ABOUT IT: Life is short, it is a breath, a fleeting shadow. What is man that God cares for him? What is man that God would sacrifice His only Son to save mankind?

Mankind is loved by God. This is an unconditional love that transcends all our rational concept of love. We can't earn it; we do not deserve it. We can only receive it with thanksgiving. It rejoices the heart of God for us to receive His gift of love and be grateful.

The Lord is our trainer, lover, fortress, deliverer, shield of refuge, and defender. He does everything 100% right for all His children. He does everything for us, not only now, but for all eternity. Our maker is our is our beloved one and we are His beloved ones.

Live your life as beloved of God. Give your life as beloved of God. Change this world by living love.

PSALM 145:3,4

Great is the Lord, and greatly to be praised; and his greatness is unsearchable. One generation shall praise thy works to another, and shall declare thy mighty acts.

KJV

THINK ABOUT IT: We have a great responsibility, to pass on the mighty acts of God from the beginning of time. He has been so mighty in His love for humankind, that His Love Story must be told throughout all generations. Our time to do that is very short, we will not pass this way again.

Every moment should be spent in declaring the greatness of the Lord to this generation, so that the generations that follow, will carry on His love and goodness to the generations that follow them.

The praise of the mighty acts of God, His work throughout all generations, is the most effective way to bring people to

Christ. The focus must be on the Lord God and His gracious goodness. It is like a cup of water to a thirsty soul. His compassion and mercy heals broken lives; His embrace brings love to the unloved. We can teach and preach by giving love to the unloved, even if it costs us our life.

I pray that next generation will return to the Lord with such passion that the whole world will be filled the Love of the Lord. Jesus is the way, the truth and the life.

Follow Him and change the world.

Your Thoughts

PSALM 146: 1-4, 9,10

Praise the LORD. Praise the LORD, O my soul. I will praise the LORD all my life; I will sing praise to my God as long as I live. Do not put your trust in princes, in mortal men, who cannot save. When their spirit departs, they return to the ground; on that very day their plans come to nothing.
The LORD watches over the alien and sustains the fatherless and the widow, but he frustrates the ways of the wicked. The LORD reigns forever, your God, O Zion, for all generations. Praise the LORD.

NIV

THINK ABOUT IT: I often struggle with whether I should trust a person. Trust has been an issue in my life, from childhood. Every time I turn around, someone or some business has been found to be untrustworthy. What do we do in this world of untrustworthiness?

I asked the Lord about what to do. He impressed on me the word of the Lord in Proverbs 3:5,6 "Trust in the Lord with all your heart and lean not unto your own understanding; in all your ways acknowledge Him and He will direct your path." Trust only the One who can save and bring you the right way. Human beings will die and their plans die with them; but the Lord God is eternal and His faithfulness is also eternal.

"The way of the wicked is turned upside down."

PSALM 146:9 KJV

It cannot stand right side up. Praise the Lord.

PSALM 147:1; 11; 5

Praise ye the LORD; for it is good to sing praises unto our GOD; for it is pleasant; and praise is comely... The LORD taketh pleasure in them that fear Him, in those that hope in His mercy... Great is our LORD, and of great power; His understanding is infinite.

KJV

A WORD FROM ME: It has been a while since I have written to you. The reason is that I was whisked away to Phoenix, to Banner Good Samaritan Hospital for brain surgery. The surgeon removed a 5 inch in diameter tumor from the left rear of my brain - IT WAS BENIGN. It seems that it had been growing there for about 10 or more years and had pushed my brain way up into the skull. This was the reason for the many falls that I had and the problems with my balance.

It was because of this experience that I have reached a greater depth in my relationship with the LORD. The whole situation was out of my hands. I didn't know the Doctor who operated on me nor anything about the Hospital that I was in, neither could I do anything to deter mine the result. Only the LORD knew all that was needed. He chose the right surgeon and the right Hospital with the right staff. He provided for my family and anointed the gifts of each member to provide for the needs of the others and myself. Yes, the LORD did it all; praise be His Holy Name forever and ever.

Why did He do all this wonderful blessing for me and my family? So that, with all that is in me, we could testify of His great love and infinite mercy. So that we could build up those who are heavy laden and turn their eyes toward the LORD with hope in their heart. So that all who hear the wonders of the LORD will turn to Him and find rest in His Love. It wasn't for us, but for His Holy Name sake. The LORD gave me a word for all people. It is a word that we all know, but do we really understand what it means. He said, "I love you first" Before anything was created, the LORD loved us as individuals. He chose us, before we ever could have chosen Him. He loved us and made it possible for us to love Him. He saved us, so that we could be with Him forever and ever. He did everything for us and all we have to do is receive His Love, JESUS Christ the LORD; receive Him in full surrender and submission.

I was unable to do anything for myself and He taught me that when I was unable to do anything, He is able to do EVERYTHING. HIS MERCY IS FROM EVERLASTING TO EVERLASTING.

There were many who said that the fact that I have no disability from the surgery and that I have progressed faster than estimated, was a miracle. No, this is only signs and wonders of the MIRACLE GOD. Not a GOD who does miracles, but the GOD who is the Miracle. Do you realize that having access to the Throne of Grace through JESUS Christ is a miracle? Do you realize that the mighty work of JESUS, reconciling us to GOD, is a miracle? Do you realize that the fact that we are breathing is a miracle from GOD, who gives us breath? When you realize that GOD is the miracle, then look all around you and you will see the signs and wonders coming from GOD. BE AMAZED, DEARLY BELOVED, BE AMAZED!!!!!

Your Thoughts

PSALM 148:11-14

Kings of the earth and all peoples; Princes and all judges of the earth; Both young men and maidens; Old men and children. Let them praise the name of the Lord, For His name alone is exalted; His glory is above the earth and heaven. And He has exalted the horn of His people, The praise of all His saints — Of the children of Israel, A people near to Him.

NKJV

HALLELUJAH!

A WORD FROM ME: As I read these verses, I was drawn to the phrase, "His Name only is exalted, His splendor is over earth and heaven."

The KJV says: "For His Name alone is excellent; His glory is above the earth and heaven."

In truth, the Messiah has come, His Name is JESUS and He

has all authority in Heaven and in the earth. There will come a time, very soon I hope, when all "alien forms of royalty, sovereignty and authority" will bow before Him, because they will recognize that they have no power. HIS NAME ONLY IS EXALTED.

Many times in the Scripture, we are admonished not to exalt ourselves. It says that those who exalt themselves will be brought low. The humble shall be exalted, because they know their rightful place in relation ship to GOD. GOD raises up the lowly, "He has raised up strength for His people," GOD raised JESUS from the dead; GOD lifts up the humble and meek. He is the HOLY ONE. As we begin a New Year, the year of our LORD, in the Jewish calendar, let us make this a year when we exalt the Name of the LORD together and sing His praises in one accord, looking to JESUS the author and finisher of our faith.

PSALM 149:1 & 150:1,2; 6

Praise ye the LORD! Sing unto the LORD a new song, and His praise in the congregationPraise ye the LORD! Praise GOD in His sanctuary; praise Him in the firmament of His power. Praise Him for His mighty acts; praise Him according to His excellent greatness....
LET EVERYTHING THAT HATH BREATH PRAISE THE LORD. PRAISE YE THE LORD!!!

KJV

IT IS by the grace of GOD that I am back at my post and can give to you the encouragement that the LORD GOD is with us. It is with highest praise that I write this Word for the Week from the Psalms, because the LORD has done great things, and Holy is His Name.

When I was admitted to the hospital in Phoenix for brain surgery, I did not know the surgeon who would remove the 5 inch in diameter tumor from my brain; I did not know the Hospital in Phoenix that I was in, nor the people who would care for me. BUT GOD KNEW THEM ALL AND ALL I HAD TO DO WAS TRUST HIM.

The surgery went very well with no disability to me at all. Even my eye sight has improved and my walking is better than it was before surgery. I am back at Church with the strength beginning to return faster than anyone ever expected, including me. GOD is in control and all I need to do is trust Him.

My New Year wish for you is that you latch on to the fact that GOD has your life in His Hand and He wants for you the very best possible. He has a plan for you, a plan to prosper you and not to harm you. He will see you through any circumstance so that you will be His sign and wonder in this world. He has given resurrection power to His people by the Holy Spirit and there is nothing that is impossible with GOD. Believe Him, Worship Him and Serve Him only; you will be blessed; HAPPY NEW YEAR, DEAR SISTERS AND BROTHERS IN CHRIST.

Thank you for your prayers, they are a cradle to rest in, Praise the LORD.

YOUR THOUGHTS:

ABOUT THE AUTHOR

I was born in Philadelphia, Pennsylvania and raised in a close-knit family. My church was a conservative, fundamental Evangelical Bible believing, teaching and preaching house of worship.

I went to Quaker School; Presbyterian College and was on the staff of three Episcopal Churches; one Presbyterian Church and am now Associate Pastor of a Church that lives its faith in word and in action.

My journey has taken me through many years in the opera and concert performance; opera and symphony management; conducting choirs orchestra; Children's music in choirs, orchestra and dramatic performance.

I spent many years bringing the arts and creativity to long term care facilities. Inspiring others to create, even in their last years.

I have 5 years of Pastoral Counseling Education and a lifetime of Biblical study and digging into the depth of God's word.

I was married to my husband for 56 years. We have 3 children all married; 6 grandchildren 5 married; 6 great grand children all babies. Each person in this family is a gift from God to me. All have given beauty to my life. I am grateful.

Rebecca Riviere

www.ingramcontent.com/pod-product-compliance
Lightning Source LLC
Chambersburg PA
CBHW071802080526
44589CB00012B/648